GW00566567

Sathya Sai's

Anugraha Varshini

(SHOWERS OF GRACE)

Sudha Aditya

PUBLISHING

© Sai Uma

ISBN. 81-86822-08-9

First Edition - 1996
Reprint - 1997

Published & Distributed by :
Sai Towers Publishing.
P.O. Box No.2, 3/497, Main Road
Prasanthi Nilayam - 515 134
Phone: 91-8555-87270, 87327, 87329, 87368
Fax   : 91-8555-87302
EMail : saitower@giasbg01.vsnl.net.in

Printed by:
D.K. Fine Art Press Pvt. Ltd.
NEW DELHI - 110 052

DIVINE MESSAGE

You cannot win My Grace through the logistics of reason, the rituals of worship, the contortions of yoga or the denials of asceticism. You can win My Grace through love alone - the love that knows no selfishness and makes no demands, the love that does no bargaining and seeks no reciprocation, the love that is unwavering, sacrificing and forgiving, the love that can overcome all obstacles and destroy all differences.

Such a love will invite My Grace in abundance and profusion; it will be *Anugraha Varshini* for now and ever more!

- Bhagavan Sri Sathya Sai Baba

A PRAYER

O' Lord! Take my love and let it flow in fullness of devotion to Thee.

O' Lord! Take my hands and let them work incessantly for Thee.

O' Lord! Take my soul and let it be merged in one with Thee.

O' Lord! Take my mind, thoughts, words and deeds and let them be in tune with Thee.

O' Lord! Take my everything and let me be Thy instrument to work.

I do but aspire to grow
In longing for Thy Lotus Feet,
And to sing Thy Holy Name
With every breath of my being.

I dedicate this book to the Lotus Feet of my Beloved Sai with love, humility and devotion.

- Sudha Aditya

CONTENTS

vi

PREFACE

Dear Sai Sisters and Brothers,

It would be incorrect to call this a sequel or a second part to my other book, "Sathya Sai's Amrita Varshini". The only similarity between them is that both have their source in the Inner Sai. But, while *"Amrita Varshini"* mainly propounds spiritual truths, this one deals with the practical application of these truths. It is a collection of teachings from our Lord Sai as to how we should face the challenges of life and become better human beings.

Most of these messages came to me from the Inner Sai during some of the most difficult and testing periods of my life. They were the mind's balm and the heart's ease, and gave me immense consolation, courage and calmness. These gems of advice and instruction are not exclusive to me. They are meant for each and everyone of us who is struggling in the cross-currents of life and is striving to reach the shores of peace and tranquillity. I know that these precious messages will touch the very core of your being and I hope, dear friends, that they will afford strength and solace to you, as they have to me.

Our Beloved Baba is our greatest refuge and our only source of joy and comfort. His words of compassion and sympathy are tender outpourings of His Divine love and are like *"Anugraha Varshini"*, showers of Grace and Blessings. We should deem ourselves infinitely blessed and fortunate that we have Him with us in person, to counsel and guide us along the winding paths of life.

I am, yours in Sai Prema and Seva.

- Sudha Aditya

THE INNER VOICE

The Inner Voice is the voice of command. It is My Divine Voice and therefore your Inner Voice is your Divine Voice. It is through this Voice that the Divine Will is expressed. What you hear and receive through this Voice is *Parama Sathyam* (the Highest Truth) and *Divya Sankalpam* (the Divine Will).

I shall tell you some more about this. You have become aware of how I function at two levels--the human plane and the Divine Plane. On the human plane I move and act like an ordinary human being. I show only the human aspect to people, But with many others, I move on a Divine plane. I reveal My Divinity to them, and My relationship with them is on a Divine plane or level. When you see Me in the darshan lines, you see My human physical form and hear My physical voice. Your speech and interaction with Me are on the human plane. This is because I am bound by many human and worldly restrictions.

When a bird is free, it flies wherever it wants, and soars to great heights. The sky is the limit. But when it builds a nest and has to live in it, it is bound by the confines of its house. Since it has

1

itself built the nest, it has to adhere to the boundaries and restrictions which are placed on it by the nest. Similarly, I too am bound on the human level. My human body is bound by the same laws and constrictions as yours. But when you sit in meditation, and are in close communion with Me through the Inner Voice, your interaction within Me is on the Divine plane. You experience Me as the vast, limitless and unbounded ocean.

These two planes are not separate and distinct. They cannot be compartmentalised. It is difficult for you to see the difference. They are like milk and water existing in the same container. They mingle and mix with each other and are not perceptible to the human eye.

Your Inner Voice exists and functions on the Divine plane. It is like a golden cord which links and binds us both together. Just as you throw a rope down to a drowning man and lift him up to safety, I use this golden cord to lift you up from the human plane to the Divine plane. When you reach the Divine plane you are in direct contact with Me. You are unaware of your external surroundings. The physical world ceases to bother you. You are in tune with Me. You are one with Me. We become one and you are Divine. At this point of time human frailties and attributes do not exist and you function on the Divine level. As you continue to meditate, over a period of time you will grow purer and finer. You will learn to extend the Divine level of consciousness to cover your waking and working states. Eventually you will begin to think, plan, work, act and function from the level of the Divine plane. This is the value and efficacy of your Inner Voice. It makes you Divine.

Therefore, listen to the Inner Voice. Always follow It and do what It tells you. Have faith and confidence in It. Have belief and trust in what It tells you. The Inner Voice is never wrong. As It expresses the Divine Will, what it tells you will ultimately prevail and come to pass. Sometimes, It may tell you something which is seemingly contrary to what I say on the human level. But, cling to the Divine Voice at all costs as you would cling to a lifeline. Because eventually, the Divine Word becomes the Will and the Will becomes the Act.

SPIRITUAL HUNGER

Weeping for material prosperity is *rajasic*, weeping for family and friends is tamasic, but weeping for God is *sathwic*. People weep and shed buckets of tears for the sake of worldly riches and for the sake of mother, father, husband, wife, brother, sister, son, daughter and so on. But very few people weep for the sake of God. Who is it that weeps for God? It is those who have a deep yearning for His Presence and a deep longing for Divine union. This spiritual hunger is the most important thing in life because it is the starting point of spiritual activity. Without hunger, can you relish a feast? Similarly, without spiritual hunger there can be no *Sadhana* (spiritual practice) and no *Sannidhi* (Divine Presence). Spiritual emotion leads to devotion, and devotion leads to God-vision (*Bhava-Bhakthi-Bhagavan*).

The tears which you shed for Me are no ordinary tears. They are as pure and sacred as *Teertha* (holy water) because they spring from the divine love and devotion in you. People go to the *Ganga* to take a dip in its holy waters and to wash away their sins. But the tears of your devotion are as pure and sacred as the water of the holy Ganga. When you shed them for Me, they will wash away all your wrongs. Your tears are like *Ganga-Jal* (Ganga Waters), worthy of washing My Feet.

4

Material wealth and worldly ties are not permanent and lasting. They are like passing clouds, here today and gone tomorrow, whereas, God is the one Person who is with you birth after birth and in all your lifetimes. He is your life companion not just in this birth but in all your past and future ones too. So, you should not bother to waste time in weeping and yearning for worldly assets and relationships. Instead, it will be better for you to weep and yearn for God. It is the right and proper thing. Therefore, develop a hunger for Him, crave for His Love, yearn for His Grace and Blessings. Your tears will melt His heart and you will verily gain Him in this way.

I AM THE SPIRITUAL DOCTOR

What do you do when your head is splitting, your body is aching and your fever is raging? You go to your family doctor or physician who examines your symptoms, diagnoses the illness and gives you the necessary medicines. You take the medicines according to his prescription and in due course you are rid of the fever and the aches and pains.

But when your mind and spirit are heavy with the burden of worries, troubles and anxieties; when your heart is longing for Me and your soul is yearning for Me; when your entire being is crying out for Me, then I am the only One who can cure you. I am the One who can ease your mind, lighten your heart and quench the thirst of your spirit. Mine is the Hand which lays cooling balm on your aching heart; Mine is the Voice which utters soothing words of comfort to your tired mind; Mine is the Love which envelops your yearning spirit and assuages its pangs of longing.

Bring to Me your mind with all its doubts and fears, uncertainties and suspicions, worries and anxieties, troubles and miseries. I know how to rid your mind of all these turmoils and give it ease. Bring to Me your heart with all its longings and emotions, thrills and ecstasies, sadnesses and despairs. I know how to treat it and give it peace. And when your

6

spirit longs and pines for Me, know that I am by your side, holding you in the warmth of My Love.

I am your Spiritual Doctor. I know how best to cure you and set you right. Love is My only cure, My only remedy. It is not sold at a chemist's store or bartered at a fair. It is there, freely and abundantly available to all and every one. The only thing is that you should make yourself capable of receiving it. In order to receive something you should have a bowl or a cup, is it not? So, let your mind and heart be like a bowl or cup to receive the sweet nectar of My Love and My Grace.

How should you turn your mind and heart into suitable receptacles? It is by cultivating "Upavasa" or closeness with Me. Develop an intimate and moment-to-moment relationship with Me. I do not want to be kept on a pedestal or altar and worshipped from afar at stipulated times. I want you to bring Me into your daily life. Talk to Me, converse with Me, joke with Me. Smile and laugh with Me, be happy with Me, be attuned to Me. Associate yourself with Me and dissociate yourself from the pursuit of worldly and material pleasures. These may give you happiness, but it will not be lasting, only passing, whereas, the happiness and peace that I give you are lasting and beyond all description.

When your mind and spirit are fatigued, turn to Me for succour; I shall renew them and give them strength and vigour. Turn only to Me at such times. Do not try to distract yourself with objective pleasures like watching a film or reading a novel or going for an outing. All these may succeed in distracting you, but they are only temporary distractions. They are not a permanent cure for the exhausted mind and spirit. They are like pain-relievers, not antibiotics. They give only momentary relief but do not cure. So, when your mind is depressed and your spirits are low, turn to Me immediately. Sit quietly in your room and contemplate or meditate on Me. If you are not able to do this, listen to *Bhajans* or sing by yourself, read some good *Sathwic* book or go out and talk to a fellow devotee. *Sathsang* helps a great deal in relieving pain. All these will give you the peace you seek and need. But above all, closeness with Me will give you the happiness and bliss you look for and long to attain.

DEPRESSION

Why do you get depressed and dejected when you are close to me? You think constantly of Me, you talk to Me, you live in close *"Upavasa" with* Me. Why then this depression? It is like being next to the fire and still feeling cold. It is like partaking of a rich feast and still feeling hungry. In both cases, the malady lies in your physical constitution and system. If you apply the suitable remedy you will be cured.

So also, when you are depressed, the fault lies within you, in your mind. You must examine yourself and diagnose your trouble. Your mind gets depressed because of three things:-

1. You may have eaten *Rajasic* or *Tamasic* food which affects the mind negatively.

2. Your mind gets involved in worldly tensions, problems, worries, anxieties and desires.

3. You may have absorbed some adverse vibrations even without your knowledge.

What is depression? It is an appendage of the mind and a trait of the ego. When your mind is free from problems and anxieties, it is happy; the ego is inflated and the mood is one of elation. But when the mind is bowed down with problems and anxieties, it is unhappy; the ego is deflated and the mood is one of dejection. So you see that dejection and depression are only states of the mind. Remove the mind. What happens then? The ego too vanishes and with it, all moods of elation and depression. You are able to remain in a mood of constant tranquillity and serenity.

How should you achieve this? The three things which cause depression are well within your control. You should not allow these to affect your mind. No doubt, problems and worries do exist but they are only transient like passing clouds. They are here today and gone tomorrow. So, what is the use of upsetting your mind and losing your peace? Worries and anxieties are like barriers between you and Me. They grip your mind so powerfully that you begin to lose the feeling of closeness with Me. And when that happens you get depressed. Depression is the result of separation from God.

Therefore, you should keep your mind in tight reins. Controlling and subduing it are in your hands. Whatever happens, keep your mind always fixed on Me. Do not let it become distracted by worldly problems. When they occur, just hand them over to Me without any hesitation. I shall tackle them for you. There is no problem in the world which is too small or too big for Me to handle. So, surrender all your problems to Me and have the confidence that I shall solve them for you. Do not worry about anything. Why fear when I am here to take care of you? When you place your burdens in My Hands, why continue to burden your mind? Your mind should be free to dwell on Me.

Empty your mind of worldly thoughts and fill it with love-My Love. Fill it with love for Me and for My children. This is what I want from you - a mind which is *Nirmal* (pure) and *Komal* (tender) and which is saturated with the sweetness and softness of divine love.

UGADI MESSAGE

What is *Ugadi*? There are two syllables in the word - "*Uga*" and "*Adi*". "*Uga*" or *Yuga* means period or year and "*Adi*" means the beginning. So *Ugadi* is the beginning of a New Year. My Message to you on this day is *Love*. Begin the New Year on the note of love and go on singing the melody of love wherever you are. All My devotees should be like candles in the darkness, spreading the light and warmth of My Love wherever they go. Love is the only force which can forge unity in mankind. There should be no room in your heart for any other emotion but love.

In your unit too, let love be the unifying force. Sink all the petty jealousies and personality clashes under the common banner of love. It is not personalities who constitute the Sai Organisations but the persons. Personalities mean egos but persons are pure sons. Every person is a reflection of Myself. The same divine spark exists in each and every one of you. So, how can there be room in your hearts and minds for petty emotions and feelings? Know yourselves as Divine, and act and behave in a divine manner. Carry the torch of love wherever you go. Love should be the hall mark of every devotee. Every devotee should be a torchbearer, lighting up all the dark corners of the world and the dark recesses of every heart. Let the entire world come together under the unifying force of *Sai Prema*. I bless you today, my dears. My Blessings will be with you in all your endeavours.

CONFIDENCE AND HUMILITY

Question:- Baba, can confidence (in God) lead to arrogance? How should we have confidence and humility at the same time?

SAI :- It is a good question that you have asked. I have already told you that devotion to God is compounded of two things-faith and confidence, It is not enough if you have mere faith in Me. You should also have confidence in Me, in My Will, Word and Act. Have faith in My Divinity and confidence in My Guardianship. "I have faith in my God, He is my only Protector and Saviour"- this should be your attitude and you should believe in Him wholeheartedly, unquestioningly and unconditionally . This is true devotion. At the same time, you should be humble in your attitude.

Never take Me for granted. That way, you will be pandering to your ego. Therefore, have faith, confidence and humility.

Now, confidence is a state of the heart while humility is a state of the mind. Confidence stems from faith in God and faith stems from the heart, whereas humility is a condition of the mind.

Think of the mind as a horse. When it is wild and untamed, it is a prey to feelings of arrogance and egoism. But once you break it in, it becomes mild, docile and calm. A tamed mind is a humble mind. Think of confidence as a jockey riding on the horse of humility. The jockey and the horse are two separate entities, but only when they ride and move as one will they reach the goal. The jockey controls, regulates and leads the horse to victory. When confidence rides on humility, you are sure to win the race and earn the Grace (of God).

Therefore, have confidence in your heart and humility in your mind. Hold on to them with all your might. I will give you many tests to try and shake you. Yesterday's was one of them. I am happy at the way in which you reacted. Never lose your confidence in Me. Be always certain that I shall look after you and solve all your problems. Have the firm belief that whatever I do is for your good and betterment. When you have this confidence you will never have any worries. Lack of confidence causes dis-ease; confidence in Me leads to peace.

SUCCESS IN LIFE-I

Success in life can be measured in two ways; one is from the material point of view and the other is from the spiritual point of view. Some people think that if they have amassed a lot of wealth and property and have earned a good name and fame they have achieved success in life. They think that the more riches they have, the more successful they are.

But, just stop and think for a minute. What is it that you take with you after you die? Do you leave this world carrying along with you, your wealth and riches? Do your material assets accompany you into the other world? No, certainly not. When you die, you leave behind all your worldly possessions and ties and take only your *Karma* and *Jnana*, that is, your actions and knowledge. Your mission in this life is to seek and discover the Truth, to realize yourself as divine, and ultimately to gain union with the Divine Being. Can this be achieved through mere material aggrandizement?

Therefore, success in life cannot be measured by the wealth and riches that you have piled up or by the name and fame that you have built up. True success in life does not depend upon your financial bank balance. What is more valuable is your spiritual bank balance. This is what counts in the eyes of God, in My view and perception. The *Atma-Jnana* (knowledge of the soul) that you achieve in this world is the highest wealth that you can hope to possess. If you have this, you are rich beyond comparison.

People may deride you and sneer at you if you do not toil after material benefits. Do not bother about them. They may scoff at you and chide you that you are wasting your life by not putting your talents to proper use. Do not heed their words. Take it from Me that no life is wasted which is dedicated to the pursuit of Truth, Reality and God. After all, this is the very purpose for which you have been born. So, if you have spiritual wealth, you can lift up your head with honour and pride and say to yourself that you are truly rich. Even if people denounce you, know that you have My backing and support.

What are most important are your own conscience and your relationship with Me. Attune your will to Mine and perform every action only with a view to pleasing Me. Then I shall be behind you completely and you shall have My full support. If the whole world praises you but you do not have My Pleasure (Approval), you are singularly bereft; if the whole world condemns you but you have My Pleasure (Approval), you are utterly blessed. My Pleasure (towards you), Approval, Blessings and Grace are more valuable than people's opinions. Ignore their idle talk and keep your mind and vision on Me.

SUCCESS IN LIFE-II

Am I always happy and cheerful? Do I have constant peace of mind? Do I possess mental equanimity at all times? Do I have a feeling of love towards everyone? These are some of the questions which you should ask yourself from time to time. The answers to these questions will tell you whether you are making progress on the spiritual path or not. If the answers to these questions are "yes" then you have certainly achieved success in life.

True success in life is not measured by worldly superiority but by spiritual superiority. Being a master in the objective world is not as important as being the master of your objective desires. Self-control and self-mastery are more important than material wealth and success. If you have a check on your worldly desires, if you have control over your senses, if you are able to remain calm and unruffled in the face of prosperity and adversity alike, if you are able to turn away from worldly attachments and turn towards God-attachment, if you have love and tolerance towards all-then you have achieved the real and true success in life.

Life has many ups and downs, peaks and troughs, elations and dejections, successes and defeats. But let me tell you one thing. It is not the actual events that are important; it is the lessons which you learn from them that are really important. It is like giving an examination paper to a class of students. Their success depends on how they tackle the questions and answer the problems. The answers are more significant than the questions. It is the answers which are evaluated and not the questions.

Similarly, many events occur in the university of life or the school of life. They may be good or bad. The test or evaluation lies in your response to the events-your behavioural response. Think of these events as University examinations and watch your responses and reactions. Life has many valuable lessons for you. So, do not turn away from it but go out bravely and meet it. Welcome its challenges gladly. Do not moan and complain. Instead, learn and mature.

The lessons of life should strengthen your moral fibre and character. You should learn to grow into a strong, sturdy tree capable of withstanding the winds of change and fortune. Just as you sharpen a knife on the whetstone, you should be able to sharpen your character on the whetstone of life. You should graduate from the University of life with honours and distinction. What are the criteria essential for your graduation? They comprise all the *Sathwic* qualities like love, tolerance, forbearance, equanimity, compassion, etc. Added to these virtues is the desire to serve the poor and the needy.

As long as you live in this world, you may be remembered and judged by your material status. But once you are dead and gone, you will be remembered only for your good works and deeds and not for your material wealth. So, remember this and act accordingly. Material prosperity brings temporary success but spiritual prosperity brings permanent success. The former gives you access (to name and fame) but the latter gives you success (in realizing God). This is real and true success because ultimately, God is the goal of human endeavour.

THE DYNAMICS OF LIFE

What you do depends on what you are. If you are world-minded you will engage only in worldly activities. If you are God-minded you will undertake Godly activities. The best thing to do is to strike a balance between the two ways of life because it is necessary to eke out a livelihood for yourself. But it should not be forgotten that the standard of life is more important than the standard of living. How you live is more important than the way you live.

It is, of course, necessary to work in order to earn a living. Work is essential so that one can live. But should one live merely to work? Millions of people the world over are so deeply engrossed in their work. They are so busy building their own little empires and kingdoms that they do not have time .for anything else. They are workaholics and their standard answer and excuse is, "I have a lot of work. I am very busy." Their lives are a constant rush of work and a whirl of activity. They do not have any time for family, friends and even for God. God, of course, occupies a low-down position in their list of priorities. He is someone to be thought of on specified days. Devotion is a uniform to be worn on certain occasions.

My dear, what sort of a life is this? An English poet once wrote:-

"What is this life so full of care,
We have no time to stand and stare."

I will modify it and put it this way-
"What is this life so full of care,
We have no time for thought and prayer."

These people who are so caught up in the whirl-pool of work-can they not keep aside a few minutes of their day for thoughts of the Divine? Can they not take off a few minutes from their time to help some poor person who is in need? Do you think these "busy" people will find real happiness and peace? They may acquit themselves and equip themselves well for this world. But do they equip themselves well for the next?

Everyone should find the time for a little intro-spection and self-analysis. Who am I? Why am I here? Where have I come from? Where am I going? What is the meaning and purpose of this life? And so on and so forth.

Life is a tool in your hands. It is an instrument through which you should learn the true meaning of living. You should *LIVE* and not merely exist. You should understand the dynamics of life and use its mechanism to gain knowledge and wisdom. Instead of that, life itself has become mechanical. Work and life are not the ends by themselves. They are only the means towards the end, the end being self and God-realization.

Therefore, master life and its ups and downs. Do not let life master you. Make your own life and do not let life make you. You can either make your life or break it. It depends upon you. If you are weak, you will sink in the ocean of life. But if you are strong, you will ride on the waves. So, be strong, be brave, be bold, be fearless, be true. Live for others and not merely for yourself. Have Me as the goal and life as the means. In this way you will surely attain Me. Herein lies the success of life.

MAKE YOURSELF STRONG

Strength of body leads to *Karma*;
Strength of mind leads to *Shanti*;
Strength of intellect leads to *Jnana*;
To all these add the sweet nectar of *Bhakti*;
And you are on the road to *Nirvana* and *Mukti*;

Keep your body always trim and in good shape. A rusty machine cannot function properly but a well-oiled and well-maintained machine will function easily, effectively and efficiently. Your body should be a fit instrument in order to perform *Karma*. Therefore, take proper care of it. Good food, sleep and exercise are all essential to keep the body fit and able. Eat moderately, sleep moderately and exercise moderately. An overdose of even one of these will throw the entire system out of gear. Remember always that health is wealth. The body is a temple of God and it is your foremost duty to take proper care of it and keep it clean, healthy and pure.

The mind is like a Pandora's Box. Open it and the monsters of desires will leap out at you and devour you. Therefore, always keep the box closed and locked securely. Throw away the key lest you may open the box inadvertently. Or better still, throw away the box itself. Then you will be ever free of desires and their attendant impulses and speculations. You will be like a still calm pool of cool serenity and blissful tranquillity.

The intellect is the purest instrument in your possession. It is the only reasoning power which discriminates and analyses-discriminates between true and false and analyses between right and wrong. Therefore, keep it razor-sharp and well-polished. All your actions and *Karmas* stem from the rational process of the intellect. Hence, keep your intellect perfectly poised and untarnished by outer elements. This will lead to maturity and wisdom.

These three-body, mind and intellect-have to be disciplined, regulated and controlled. But in order to direct these along the path to *Mukti* and *Nirvana*, you need to have love and devotion for God. It is *Bhakti* which activates you, which motivates you; *Bhakti* is your petrol. Think of yourself as a train going along the tracks of *Nirvana*. Your body is the compartment moving on the wheels of *Karma* drawn by the engine of your mind. Your intellect is the engine-driver and the fuel is *Bhakti*. Realize this truth and act accordingly.

FORGIVENESS

When you beg forgiveness of your parent, friend, brother or sister, you say "Please pardon me" or "Please excuse me" or "I am sorry, forgive me." The same word *Forgive* when used in relation to God assumes a special significance. When you ask God for forgiveness, there is a deeper meaning attached to the word "forgive". "For" is "fore" which means first or foremost. "Give" is surrender. So, you have to first surrender yourself completely to God and then He will bless you with His Grace.

Take the word *"Kshamarpana"* which means forgiveness. *"Kshamarpana"* is really two words- *"Kshama"* and *"Arpana"*. *"Arpana"* means to give up or surrender. The word *"Kshama"* has three syllables- Ka, Sha and Ma. *"Ka"* denotes *Karma* or action; *"Sha"* denotes *Sharira* or body' *"Ma"* denotes *Manas* or mind. So *"Kshamarpana"* (forgiveness) really means the total surrender of the body, mind and act to God. When you ask Me sincerely and wholeheartedly for forgiveness, it is actually an act of surrender. And when you give up your body, mind and action to Me, I have to shower My Grace on you.

I AM YOUR CARETAKER

In life you should not be careworn but carefree;
In living you should not be careless but careful;
In worldly affairs you should be uncaring but
    with people you should be caring.
But most of all, in everything I am your
    Caretaker.

Firstly, you should not allow yourself to be worn
down by the ups and downs of life. You should not
be elated by praise and success; you should not be
dejected by blame and failure. Happiness and joy,
sorrows and disappointments are a part and parcel
of life but they should not affect your mental state.
Whatever life hands out to you, you should learn to
accept it with unruffled calm and cheerfulness.
You should maintain your equanimity and equipoise
at all times and in all situations. Your mind will
then be free of all entanglements and burdens. You
will not be worn down by cares, you will be free of
them.

The second aspect deals with your manner of
living, that is the codes of conduct and the norms of
behaviour. See good, hear good, speak good, think
good, do good, be good. These are the cardinal rules
for righteous living. Above all, mind your tongue.
The tongue is enemy number one of man. Three
things are associated with the tongue-taste, talk and

27

temper. All these three should be controlled. You should not be careless, lest the tongue may commit even one error. When the foot trips and slips, much harm may not be caused but when the tongue trips and slips, the damage and harm may be irreparable. Therefore, be cautious and careful and guard against any little lapse.

Thirdly, you should be uncaring about worldly things. That is, you should not be much affected by worldly achievements and successes, name, fame, power and glory. And it is right that it should be so because attachment to worldly things only causes unrest. So it is right that you should not care about them. But when it comes to people, you should be caring and loving. Man is a reflection of God, so learn to extend your love to all. You must have love for everyone, compassion for the suffering, and sympathy for the destitute. Love all, serve all-let this be your motto in life.

But above all, remember always that I am your caretaker. That is to say, I take away your cares and I also take care of you. When I am here to carry all your burdens and cares, why should you have worry and anxiety? I shall relieve you of all your problems and difficulties, troubles and sorrows. There is no problem which is too small or too big for Me to handle. Just as a housewife turns her hand willingly to any chore however menial or monumental, I shall bear all your burdens big and small. There is no work which is beneath Me, no problem which is insignificant for Me. Therefore, rid yourself of the weight of your cares for I am there to carry them. Your mind will then be light and free.

I also take care of you at all times and in all places. *"Yogakshemam Vahaamyaham"*. I bear the burden of your welfare, both material and spiritual. I am always walking by your side with one arm supporting you and the other guiding you. And when you are in pain, I even carry you. Know that I am always beside you, watching over you and protecting you. I am your Divine Caretaker. Therefore, rid yourself of all burdens, throw away all your cares and step forth lightly on to the stage of life with *Ananda* and *Shanti*.

RAMANAVAMI MESSAGE

All of you celebrate *Ramanavami* as the day when Sri Rama incarnated in this world. But do you know what the festival actually means, spiritually and morally? There is an inner significance to *Ramanavami* which few realize and understand. I shall tell you what this inner meaning is.

When you consider the name "*Rama*", it consists of two syllables, "*Ra*" and "*Ma*". These two syllables denote something very important. The syllable "*Ra*" stands for Ravana and the syllable "*Ma*" for "*Mardana*" (destroyer). Ravana was a person with immense egoism, arrogance, anger and desire. He symbolises the *Rajoguna* (*rajas*) which includes all these vices. Just as Sri Rama humbled Ravana and destroyed him, the spiritual aspirant too should aspire to get rid of the *Rajoguna*. This *Guna* is a serious handicap and impediment in the path of the *Sadhaka*. Therefore, every *Sadhaka* should try to subdue and destroy the *Rajoguna* which is present within. The day you succeed in this is true *Ramanavami* -the birth of a new and pure person. You need not destroy all the *Rajasic* traits at the same time. That will not be possible. It is enough if you take up one at a time and try to destroy it. In this way, you will be able to celebrate *Ramanavami* with sincerity and dedication.

30

When we talk about the story of Rama, there is one more important fact which one should remember. When Sita saw the golden deer in the forest and desired to possess it, what happened? It led to her separation from Rama and this caused her untold misery and suffering. The real significance of this is that as long as you have desires for and attachments to worldly objects, you can never have true peace and happiness. Attachment to objective pleasures only causes unrest. True and lasting peace and happiness can be obtained only when you have attachment to God. Therefore, detach yourself from worldly desires and attach yourself to God. This way lies permanent peace and bliss. This is the real meaning and message of *Rama Katha*.

ADJUSTMENT SADHANA

When I'm with you, never fear.
You are to Me so precious and dear.
Don't take things to heart so severe.
Be always happy, smiling and of good cheer.
Your *Karma* and your *Seva* now hold you here.
Take them as your *Sadhana* and do most
    revere.
Missing My *Darshan* causes you many an
    unhappy tear,
But remember, *Karma Yogis* and *Sevakas*
    are to Me very near!

My dear! Life is like a long journey. Man is like a car travelling on the road of life. There are scores of people travelling on the same road.

When you set out on the road, you see so many cars, buses, trucks, vehicles etc. on the same route. Do you think that the entire road belongs to you and that you can drive just as you please? No, of course not. You have to drive with care and caution and adjust your car to accommodate all the other vehicles on the road. Also, you have to observe the rules and regulations of the traffic. Otherwise, there will be accidents. In short, you have to keep manoeuvring your car carefully, constantly adjusting it and accommodating it in order to avoid clashes and disasters.

Similarly, in life also you have to adjust and accommodate yourself to people, situations and circumstances and the needs arising from them. A housewife will have many kinds of household chores, all sorts of duties and hundred types of responsibilities. She has to organise herself carefully and adjust herself to meet the various needs of her family and household. But the important thing is that she should organise herself in such a way that she does not get totally immersed in the household chores. She should not be bowed down by the weight of her duties. She should carry her responsibilities joyfully, willingly and cheerfully, and discharge them in such a way that she has some time of her own for her personal *Sadhana* and prayer.

As a householder, a hundred things may arise during the course of the day which hinder your *Sadhana*. These unexpected duties may impinge upon your meditation and prayer time. For instance, you may have finished all your work and just as you are settling down for meditation, there is a knock on the door and guests come in. Will you scold them and chase them away because they have prevented you from your prayer? Certainly not. Instead, you will welcome them cheerfully, talk to them warmly and make them feel at home. Remember the saying "*Athithi Devo Bhavah*". (The guest is like God). So you treat the guests politely, and in this way think that you are serving God Himself.

So also, regarding your daily duties too, the usual and the unusual, the ordinary and the extra-ordinary-don't think of them as obstructions and hindrances to your *Sadhana*. If you think of them as such, they will become a burden and sit heavily on you. You will feel worn down by them. But if you think of them as part of worship, they will sit lightly on you and you will not even notice their weight. Duty is devotion and work is worship. So, take everything as a form of *Sadhana*. Whatever you have to do, however mundane, irksome or irritating, think that you are doing them for Me. Every little adjustment and accommodation that you have to make will become a *Sadhana* the moment you say to yourself". This is not for me, it is for Sai. I'm not doing this for anyone else, I'm doing it for Baba." This is adjustment *Sadhana* and in time you will be able to do everything cheerfully and without resentment.

When you go to *Prasanthi Nilayam* during a festival, you have to sit in such a cramped fashion and adjust yourself as comfortably as possible in a foot of space. But, do you complain, do you groan? You accept the discomfort cheerfully because you think of it as a *Sadhana*. You are prepared to put up with anything for My sake. You will bear anything for the sake of My *Darshan*.

Then, why not have the same attitude in your daily life? Put up with every little inconvenience with good cheer, bear every little discomfort with a smile. You are doing everything for Me, for My sake and in order to please Me. This kind of adjustment *Sadhana* should become part of your worship and prayer. It is *Nishkama Karma* itself and it will please Me tremendously.

ANUGRAHA AND KARUNA
(Grace and Mercy)

Today I shall tell you the difference between
Anugraha (Grace) and *Karuna* (Mercy).

What exactly does "*Karuna*" mean? The syllable *Ka* denotes "*Kaivalya*" meaning heavenly or
divine. *Runa* means debt. So the word "*Karuna*"
means divine debt. What is this debt? Who owes
this debt and to whom? The answer is quite simple,
The debt is the one which God owes to His devotee.
The debt is nothing but the Lord's urge to save His
devotee from misery and suffering. God is *Karuna
Sagara*, the ocean of mercy. When the devotee calls
out to Him for help, He is duty-bound to rush at
once to the devotee's aid. Just as the mother runs to
the child when the child cries piteously for her, the
Lord too rushes to the devotee's side when he calls
out to Him helplessly. This is the bond which exists
between *Bhakta* and *Bhagavan* - a bond which binds
Bhagavan and constrains Him to respond immediately to the *Bhakta's* cry. But this cry should come
straight from the depths of the heart and should not
be tainted by any feeling of egoism or pride. Only
if the cry is pure, sincere and heartfelt can it melt
the heart of the Lord and make Him respond.

Now, "*Anugraha*" as you know, means "grace". *Anu* means "good" and *Graha* means "time or period". So "*Anugraha*" means blessings for a good life. The only person who can give you this blessing of assurance is God Himself. It is not easy to earn this blessing and secure Divine Grace. The reason is that when God bestows His Grace, He looks at your *Samskaras* in the past, present and future. He takes into account your good thoughts and deeds both in the past and in the present birth. Depending upon your *Samskaras*, He chooses the appropriate time to shower His Grace. You cannot see your *Samskaras* but they are all recorded in your Spiritual Account Book and He can see all your debits and credits. So He alone knows when and how He should extend Grace to you.

Of course, there are persons who, by their great devotion, draw the Lord's Grace upon them, irrespective of their *Samskaras*. The sheer power of their devotion cancels out all their negative *Samskaras* and attracts the Lord's Grace and Blessings. But such devotees are rare and few in number.

Therefore, when you pray to God, pray for His Mercy rather than for His Grace. It is easier to obtain His Mercy than His Grace because when God shows Mercy, He does so out of His infinite Compassion and pity regardless of your *Samskaras*, *Karmas* and whatever you have done. So, pray for His *Karuna*,

His *Kripa* and His *Daya*. Melt His heart by the warmth of your cry, the sincerity of your prayer and the anguish of your soul. The depth and strength of your prayer will move Him to compassion. And this is very important for you. For, *Anugraha* may show you the road to happiness but *Karuna* helps you to walk along it. *Anugraha* may give you a good life but *Karuna* helps you to live.

KRISHNASHTAMI MESSAGE

Sri Krishna was born on the 8th night of the full moon. *Krishnashtami* or *Janmashtami*, as some people call it, is celebrated as Sri Krishna's birthday. Is it an ordinary birthday like so many others? No, it is special because it is rich in spiritual truths and fraught with high philosophy. The word *"Krishnashtami"* holds a meaning which is far more significant than just the day of birth. This word can be split into three smaller words-Krishna, *Ashta* and Mi. *Krishna* means dark and denotes the dark side of human nature. *Ashta* means eight and denotes the eight lesser or base qualities present in man. *Mi* is *"Mithya"* which means false or unreal. The word *Krishnashtami*, therefore, tells us that there are eight base qualities, traits or vices which form the dark side of man; these qualities are false and unreal because they do not represent the true and real nature of man which is Divinity.

What are these eight vices? They are *Kama* (desire), *Krodha* (anger), *Lobha* (greed), *Moha* (attachment), *Mada* (egoism), *Matsarya* (jealousy), *Ajnana* (ignorance) and *Maya/Branthi* (delusion). These qualities cloud man's inner perception and prevent him from realizing the truth of his inherent divinity. Just as the clouds obscure the sun and shut out the light, these qualities obscure man's inner vision and shut out the light of *Jnana* (knowledge).

Therefore, it is the duty of every *Sadhaka* to subdue the dark side of his nature and bring it out into the light-from *Krishna Paksha* to *Sukla Paksha* ie., from darkness to light. The day after *Krishnashtami* is celebrated as *Krishna Jayanthi*. "*Jayanthi*" means "victory" and *Krishna Jayanthi* means victory over the dark side of your self. So, the day you are able to achieve victory over your "dark self" is true *Krishna Jayanthi*. Realize the deep inner significance of this important festival and understand the lesson it holds for you. Practise what it preaches and move from darkness towards light, from ignorance to knowledge.

There is another lesson which Lord *Krishna's* birth teaches us. *Krishna* was born at midnight within the four walls of a prison. But his father, *Vasudeva*, carried the Divine child away from the prison, walking all through the night to *Mathura*. On his hazardous journey, he met with many obstacles which he overcome by the Grace of the Lord. Through the Lord's Grace, the prison doors opened by themselves and the prison guards fell asleep, thereby enabling *Vasudeva* to walk out unhindered. Later, he reached the river *Yamuna* and, again by the Lord's Grace, walked over it. And thus, he reached the house of *Nanda* and *Yasoda* in the morning.

Now, let us consider the spiritual significance behind this. When man is born into this world, his true nature is imprisoned within the walls of the mind and the ego. But with the help of *Jnana* (*Vasudeva*), he can free himself from imprisonment and travel towards *Sathya* (*Nanda*) and *Prema* (*Yasoda*). And in the process, he will earn the Grace and Blessings of God.

These, therefore, are the two important lessons which *Krishna's* birth teaches you. Understand them and put them into practice. Then "*Jayanthi*" will be yours.

PRAKRITI IS SUNDARAM
(Nature is Beauty)

Of all things in creation, *Prakriti* (Nature) is closest to Me because it is pure and unspoiled. It is therefore very easy to see Me in *Prakriti*. When you enjoy and appreciate the beautiful things in *Prakriti*, you are actually adoring God.

You know that there are three worlds. They are the causal (super consciousness), subtle (astral) and gross (Prakriti). The attributes of these three worlds are *Sathyam* (Truth), *Shivam* (Joy/auspiciousness), and *Sundaram* (Beauty), respectively. God is *Sathyam*, *Shivam* and *Sundaram*. *Prakriti* is *Sundaram*. So *Prakriti* itself is God.

God exists in each and every atom and particle of *Prakriti* - in every plant, tree, leaf, flower and fruit. It is therefore quite meaningless to offer these things to Me. What is the sense in offering to Me what is already Mine? Besides, why should you denude a plant of its flowers? Don't you beautify your body with *Kumkum* and ornaments? Without the ornaments, your body is denuded of its beauty. Flowers are the ornaments of the plants. Without the flowers, the plant is denuded of beauty. Is it not wrong and cruel to spoil this beauty? You should learn to love and adore Me through the beautiful things in Nature. Worship Nature and you worship God.

42

If you wish to offer Me flowers, then offer to Me your *Hrudaya Pushpam* - the flower of your heart. Make it as pure and tender as a flower, fragrant with *Sathwic* qualities, and offer it to Me. There is no greater offering which you can make to Me and no greater offering which would please Me more.

Instead of the fruit from the tree, give Me your *Karma Phala* - the fruit of your actions. Learn to do things for My sake and not for the sake of reward. Perform your actions without thinking about the results. This itself will lead to purity of mind.

If you wish to decorate and beautify My photo, do it with artificial flowers. You are not hurting *Prakriti* by offering these to Me. Your aesthetic sense will be satisfied, you create an attractive atmosphere and at the same time the plant preserves its beauty. Therefore, my dear, look for Me in every flower and fruit. Look at the flower on the plant and say, "God, how pure and tender and beautiful You are, how fragrant, how charming, how delightful!" Doesn't a flower remain more fresh and beautiful on the plant than at My photo? Beauty should be preserved and cherished, for Beauty is God and God is Beauty.

THE FIVE D'S

Depression, Dejection, Despondence, Despair, Distress - these are the Five D's which should not exist in your vocabulary at all. They should not even touch the mind of a Sai *Bhakta*. How can you experience such feelings when your mind is full of Me? When your mind is full of thoughts of Me, of love for Me, there should be no room for any negative emotions, feelings and thoughts.

There is a saying in English that empty vessels sound much. I will add that monkey minds lose their equipoise. The mind frolics to and fro like a playful monkey, attaching itself first to this pleasure and then to that, just as a monkey jumps from branch to branch. It tries to find satisfaction and fulfilment through sensory objects and worldly pleasures like seeing films, going to parties and clubs, drinking, gambling, smoking etc. But these so-called worldly pleasures are like water bubbles. They are attractive and tempting when they are new but once they burst, what remains? Nothing.

Material pleasures may give you temporary distraction but they cause permanent detraction. Now, what does this mean? It means that the mind derives only a temporary and passing satisfaction from material pleasures; but in the process it becomes a permanent prey to these very same pleasures. They grip the mind so powerfully that the mind is unable to free itself. The mind is detracted and led away from the Godward path and lured into the worldly path.

When the mind travels along the worldly path, it becomes entangled and enmeshed amidst desires, attachments and pleasures. The mind craves enjoyment, satisfaction and fulfillment from the objective world, and when it does not obtain them it is thrown into a state of disappointment and unrest. The mind seeks pleasure and happiness in possessions, relationships and attachments and when it loses them, it slips into a state of disillusionment, sorrow and grief. And thus the mind becomes the victim of various negative moods like depression, dejection, despondence, despair and distress.

Therefore, use your intellect and your reasoning power and take a firm grip over the mind. Do not let it dart here and there and pick up negative vibrations. These are harmful and adverse and are easily absorbed by the mind. So, put a chain round its neck and hold the chain firmly in your hand. Tame the monkey mind. Train it to become *Sathwic*. Feed it with devotional music and *Bhajans*, good uplifting literature, *Sathsang* and contemplation of God. Fill it with the sweet melody of love and the fragrance of devotion. Teach it to look inward and not outward. Then you will not be beset by any of the five D's. Instead, you will be re-set with eternal and unshakable happiness, bliss and peace which the Lord's Grace will bestow on you.

65th BIRTHDAY MESSAGE
(Devotee and Disciple)

My dear! My message to you on this day is very simple. It is not enough if you have mere devotion. It is more important that you should have discipline. I want all My devotees the world over to realize this significant truth. One who has devotion is called a devotee. One who has discipline is called a disciple. But, who is a devotee and who is a disciple? You may think that both are the same but you can take it from Me that there is an ocean of difference between the two.

Devotion is love, adoration and attachment towards the Lord. Discipline stems from spiritual practice, austerity and *Sadhana*. It denotes complete self-control and self-mastery. While devotion is an attitude of the heart, discipline is an attitude of the mind. It is very easy to have devotion but it is not so easy to have discipline because the mind is like a wayward monkey and it is difficult to tame and subdue it. And yet, herein lies the test of true devotion. For, it is devotion alone which leads to discipline. It is devotion which is born first; discipline develops later. Devotion gives rise to discipline.

As I said, "devotee" comes from "devotion" and "disciple" comes from "discipline". Now, I shall tell you the difference between a devotee and a disciple.

A devotee thinks of himself and God as two separate entities. To him, it is "You and I". A disciple, on the other hand, does not think of himself and God as separate entities. To him everything is "You". "Only you, not I ", he thinks constantly. There is only one entity in his vision-God, who is his Guru.

Secondly, a devotee may have intense love for God but he may not have crossed the ego boundary which separates *Bhakta* from *Bhagavan*. He is bound by the limitations which are placed on him by the ego and is hence unable to experience the vast potential of the spirit. On the other hand, a disciple has crossed the ego-boundary and has shed the shackles imposed on him by the ego. He is not restricted by any frontiers and is free to feel and experience the totality of the spirit.

Thirdly, a devotee may not possess a sense of complete surrender to the Lord. He still has a sense of *"Thine"* and *"mine"*. To him, the Lord's Will and his individual will are separate and distinct, whereas a disciple develops an attitude of complete surrender to the Lord who is his *Sadguru*. He has no sense of *"Thine* and *mine"*. To him, everything is "only *Thine"*. He does not feel that he possesses a will of his own. He thinks that everything is his Lord's Will. It does not matter to him that he has no will. It is enough for him to know that the Will of the One he loves and adores is fulfilled.

A devotee may not transfer his allegiance to the Lord unconditionally. Other relationships come in the way and deter him from seeking the Lord as the only One without a second. But to a disciple, his Divine Lord and Master are the One and the Absolute. All other worldly relationships take second place for him. Moreover, he accepts the Will of his *Sadguru* without any questions, complaints or calculations.

A devotee expects and seeks the fruit of his devotion but a disciple does not look for any reward. He is engaged in faithfully and blindly carrying out the advice and instructions of his Master, and is not troubled about the end results. To him, performance gains precedence over prize.

A devotee may yet find himself bound by the dictates and dictums of the society and of the world. But a disciple is not in any way concerned with them. To him, the Word and Will of his Lord come first, and are more important than any social and worldly regulations and requirements. His most imperative goal and task is to carry out the Wish, Word and Will of his Divine Guru.

So this, my dear, is the difference between a devotee and a disciple. You will realize from what I have told you that a disciple's status is superior to and more elevated than a devotee's. However, one fact should also be clearly recognised here. In order to become a good disciple, it is necessary to be a devotee first. Only when one has love and attachment for God does one develop the incentive and urge to practise discipline. Devotion leads to discipline. A true and sincere devotee should learn to discipline himself according to His Lord's teachings and become a good disciple. Through *Sadhana* a *Bhakta* should become a *Sishya*. This is the surest test of pure devotion. The highest *Bhakta* - the *Parama Bhakta* - is one who is also a perfect disciple of the Lord. He will be acknowledged by Me as the greatest disciple, a *Paramasishya*. I want each one of My devotees to strive towards this goal and I bless you that you shall succeed.

LOVE AND LIFE

Love lives by giving, forgiving and forgetting.
Life lies in searching, realizing and practising.

Love is a precious gift given by God to man. It is man alone who is capable of experiencing the magnitude and richness of genuine love. What is genuine love? It is that love which is selfless and unselfish, which does not expect anything in return; it is that love which is given spontaneously, whole-heartedly, unreservedly and unconditionally without any thought of self-aggrandisement; it is that love which finds pleasure, happiness and joy merely in giving, and giving freely and lavishly without seeking a reward. This is true love, this is pure love, this is *Divine Love.*

When we talk of "*Giving*", what exactly is it that we give out of our love? Is it wealth, is it riches, is it worldly possessions, financial securities or material assets? It is no hardship for a million-aire to give or distribute money and riches. It is easy to be generous with material wealth, properties and assets. Monetary or financial charity is easy, convenient and less strenuous. It is always easy to be generous and lavish with something which you possess in abundance.

But, I tell you that there is something else that you possess which is far more valuable than your

50

worldly possessions-and that is your *Self*. Giving yourself to others is more important, more worthwhile and more fulfilling. How do you give yourself? In the word *SELF*, the letters S,E,L and F stand for **S**ympathy, **E**quanimity, **L**ove and **F**ortitude. These are the four richest qualities that you can share and give to everyone around you. When a person is sick or sorrowful, show sympathy. When a spirit is restless or uneasy, give equanimity. When a heart is unhappy or miserable, shower love. When a mind is depressed or distressed, extend fortitude.

My dear, giving yourself is the greatest *Seva* which you can ever hope to engage in. It is the most difficult *Seva* but the most enriching and satisfying.

Next is *Forgiving*. There is a saying that to err is human, to forgive divine. When God can pardon and forgive even the worst criminal, why can't you? When love is pure and selfless, forgiveness is natural and spontaneous. There should be no room in your heart for petty emotions like resentment, rancour, bitterness, anger, vindictiveness or vengefulness. These feelings are not in keeping with your true nature, which is love. Therefore, be generous and charitable towards everyone. Do not try to sit in judgement over others. You have no right to criticise, condemn or censure. Only God can do that.

Now we come to *Forgetting*. What is it that you should forget? I say : forget the harm that others have done to you; forget the good that you have done to others. If you do so, your ego will not be affected. Otherwise, it will get deflated or inflated and this will lead to further impulses, desires, etc. Therefore, learn to forgive and forget.

When your love learns to give, forgive and forget totally and wholeheartedly, it becomes pure and divine. When you begin to experience this selfless divine love, then life itself takes on a new meaning and a new dimension.

What is life? What is its purpose, what is its goal? Why have I been born? Where have I come from? Where am I going? These are some of the questions you have to ask yourself constantly. Thus, life begins anew with the quest for truth and the search for your identity. Everyone, at some time or the other in his life, develops a thirst for truth and a hunger for the highest knowledge. For how long can a fish swim on the surface of the water without diving back into the depths? For how long can you play with the froth and the bubbles without reaching below for the substance? Once the froth dissolves and the bubbles burst, what remains? Just the clear water. Life is also like this. The clear pure truth is hidden under layers of illusion, delusion and worldly desires. Once these are removed, the Truth reveals itself.

Constant inquiry (*Vichaara*) into the truth , and discrimination (*Viveka*) between the real and unreal, truth and untruth, right and wrong will put you on the path of realization. Once you gain realization of your true self and identity as well as of the relationship between you and God, you will recognise and appreciate the true significance of life and the real reason for which you have been born. Life takes on a new meaning and a new purpose; you set for yourself a new aim and a new goal. Towards which end? Towards God, naturally. He becomes your new goal and you begin your journey towards Him. With this changed perception, you begin to experience a sense of unity and totality within yourself, a vision of expanded consciousness and a feeling of unparalleled bliss and peace. In this way, you are well and truly on your way up in life, with both your feet planted securely on the spiritual ladder of success. Thus, you move from seeking and searching to realising and experiencing.

The last stage of your life lies in practising. Once you discover and realize the truth, you have to learn to put it into practice. You have to spread the light of truth, the warmth of love, the ecstasy of bliss and the stillness of peace. Be like a lamp in the darkness, dispelling the gloom of ignorance and misery with its light. Be like the sun, radiating the warmth and energy of love to all around you. Be like the moon, shedding the pure and cool beams of bliss and peace to each and everyone. Love all and serve all. The ultimate urge of a spiritually evolved person is the desire to serve humanity and to help alleviate the suffering of mankind. Service to man is service to God.

If you live according to these ideals, then you have made your life worth living. If not, you have not really lived at all.

THE PHILOSOPHY OF ACCEPTANCE

When you are disappointed, you sigh.
When you are unhappy you cry.
When you lose something you groan.
When you lose somebody you mourn.
You think life treats you unfair,
And you chafe and churn beyond compare.
"Why did this happen to me", you rail.
"Fate is unkind to me", you wail.
This is the sad truth of the human tale!

Anandaswaroopa ! You feel happy and elated when life is fine and smooth; you feel unhappy and dejected when life is not so fine and smooth. When things go wrong , you rave and rant at Fate or Destiny and even at God. You turn on Him with bitter accusations . "Why did this have to happen to me?" you storm. "Why does Fate always make me suffer?" you seethe.

My dear, shall I tell you why you respond in this manner? It is because you have not learnt the philosophy of acceptance. You expect certain things from life and you are not prepared or willing to accept anything which falls short of your expectations. When you do not get what you wish for and hope for, you suffer a mental and physical upset. But let me tell you that this attitude of expecting something from life is itself wrong. It is only when you have put something into life that you can expect good rewards. Can you walk into a department store and demand something free of cost? Certainly not, you have to pay for it. In a similar manner, it is only when you have invested something worthwhile in life that you can expect a just return. Sometimes, you may not get what you think you deserve. You say, "I have not done anything bad in this life, then why should this catastrophe or calamity befall me?" Yes, you may not have done anything bad; but have you done anything good? Being negatively good is not enough, you have to be positively good too. Then again, has it not occurred to you that the reason for your suffering may lie in any one of your previous births? All debts have to be repaid at some time or the other. This is the law of *Karma*. You cannot escape it or get round it. The only way is to face it and accept it.

When you go to the temple, you stretch out your hand for the prasadam which the priest is going to give you. You do not know what he is going to give you, but nevertheless your hand is stretched out to accept it. The prasadam may be something which you normally do not like, but in the temple you accept it with reverence as the Lord's Blessing. You should try and extend this attitude to life also. Learn to accept whatever life metes out to you, whether good or bad, pleasant or unpleasant.

You should train yourself to accept the vicissitudes of life philosophically. Life is a mixture of pleasure and pain. Pleasure is the interval between two pains; pain is the interval between two pleasures. Neither pleasure nor pain lasts for ever. They are like passing clouds, here one minute and gone the next. Then why allow them to upset you at all? The best way would be to get neither deflated nor inflated, but to have an attitude of calmness and coolness, of equipoise and equanimity. Then, nothing will shake you or throw you out of gear.

I have often told you that life is a challenge and you should meet it. When there is a challenge or a wager between two people, one person lays down the challenge and the other accepts it and agrees to carry it through. In the same fashion, life throws many challenges in your path. You should accept them all sportingly and cheerfully and try your best to meet them and deal with them successfully.

Acceptance is half the battle won. Therefore, do not try to resist the inevitable. Resistance retards your progress. If you have ever tried to swim against the current, you will know what a difficult feat it is. If you have ever tried to run against the wind, you will know what an arduous task it is. In both cases, you are resisting the natural flow and your resistance is an impediment to your progress. When you try to ride your lifeboat against the tides of fortune, you will not gain anything. Instead, you will merely tire yourself out and invite despondency, dejection and despair. On the other hand, turn your lifeboat right around and ride it with the tide and you will find it sailing along smoothly and effortlessly.

So, my dear, accept and act accordingly. Whatever be your loss or disappointment, accept it philosophically as your just dues. Do not brood and grieve. You will gain nothing by lamenting over what has happened and passed. Life is like a screen. The images come and go continuously. They flow constantly without a gap or a pause. Similarly, life too is a continuous flow. You have to flow along with it. You cannot stop life from going on. You have to go along with it. What has passed is in the past. There is no use in looking back. You must only look forward.

The time for action is *Now*, in the present. At least from now engage yourself in good actions and noble deeds, and for your future births, sow some good seeds. For, as you sow, so shall you reap. Make good use of life's opportunities and options. There is always an opportunity around the corner, waiting for you. It is up to you to take it and use it for your progress. Options in life are never scarce. You have to use your discrimination to choose the best one which will help you to take you up the ladder of success. Make the best use of the means at your disposal and work towards the end.

Have discrimination, determination and discipline as your tools. They will surely help you to build your life strongly, securely and satisfactorily. Have faith in yourself and in your ability to face any storm unflinchingly. Be like the tree which bends with the breeze but does not break. Be brave and life can never defeat you. You will be the victor and the ultimate reward will be yours.

MARRIAGE IS A SPIRITUAL LADDER

What is marriage? It is no ordinary coming together of a man and a woman. It is a bond which is sealed, a union which is forged between them. Marriage means the union of body, mind and heart. A perfect mingling of these three will make a perfect and ideal marriage.

Union of the bodies or physical union is, of course, an essential and necessary part of the institution of marriage. It is necessary for procreation which is a law of Nature.

Union of the minds is the mental affinity which exists between the husband and wife. It refers to a mingling of ideas, values, standards, norms, ideals, etc. Sometimes, a husband and wife may start their married life with different mental outlooks and wavelengths. But gradually, with a patient and determined effort on both their parts, they can change their minds and put them on the same course. This can be done by reading good literature, partaking in cultural works, moving in sathsang (holy company), attending discourses by learned men and so on. These will help the minds to imbibe the correct values and ideals in life and will help them to develop the spirit of *vichaara* (inquiry) and *viveka* (discrimination). In course of time, both minds will be controlled and brought to think along the same lines.

The third is union of the hearts or emotional union. This denotes the emotions and feelings that are associated with the heart. For a successful emotional union, the important qualities are selfless love, understanding, tolerance, compassion, generosity, kindness, gentleness, thoughtfulness and forgiveness. These will not always come automatically on their own. They have to be cultivated, nurtured and fostered like tender saplings. Once the husband and wife realize and recognise the true values and ideals of life, they will strive to acquire the right qualities and attributes that are necessary for building up a strong emotional union.

A perfect harmony between husband and wife physically, mentally and emotionally will not only make a happy marriage but will also make a happy home. Parents who are united in peace and harmony will be able to project these same feelings to their children also. They will be able to create the right and proper environment for their children who will be able to acquire and develop the right and proper values in life.

It is a very sad thing that the true purpose of marriage is lost to the modern mind. If you ask the young man and woman of today as to why they get married, one may say it is because it is the accepted and expected thing in society. Another may say it is for acquiring social status, yet another may think it is for financial betterment or security. Some think it is a solution to the problem of caring for aged parents, and some even think it is an insurance against old-age loneliness! But who, nowadays, ever realizes or even thinks of the true purpose and significance of marriage?

I will tell you what it is. Marriage is for spiritual upliftment. It is not a social ladder, it is a spiritual ladder. The wife is the left side of the husband; the husband is the right side of the wife. Before marriage, they are only half-body (*ardha*). But after marriage, together they are full body. The husband is "*ardhangi*" and the wife is "*ardhangini*". Together, they form a whole and complete entity. The husband is *Shiva* and the wife is *Shakti*. They should, together, hand in hand, strive for spiritual growth.

Our ancient rishis understood very well the spiritual meaning of marriage. Great sages like Anasuya and Attreya, Ahalya and Gouthama, helped each other along the path of spiritual knowledge. The ultimate goal is the Creator and the ultimate purpose of life is to go back to the Creator. Therefore, it is the sacred duty of the husband and wife to help each other, guide and correct each other and encourage each other in their spiritual *sadhana*. Together, they should walk along the spiritual path and practise *sadhana* to enable them to acquire *self-realisation* and ultimate union with the Divine. This is the real meaning of marriage. It is a bridge between humanity and divinity on which the husband and wife walk in union and harmony.

THE TRUE MARRIAGE

Many times you would have heard Me say in the darshan line, *"Shaadi Karo"* (Get married). When I say this to married ladies and widows, they are naturally shocked and puzzled. They are shocked because they do not understand the inner significance of these words. I do not say anything without a reason; I do not utter a single word without an objective. Every word and every act of Mine has a definite purpose and a specific meaning.

I shall tell you the true significance of these two words - "Get married". It is really quite simple and is not very difficult to understand. The true marriage is the union between you and God, between your inner self and your Highest Consciousness, between *jivatma* and *Paramatma*. Your purpose in life is to go back to the One who created you. You came from pure consciousness and you have to go back to pure consciousness. In fact, you are even now pure consciousness, although you have lost sight of this knowledge. But this is only a temporary amnesia, a temporary aberration.

Therefore, when I say "Get married", it is merely to remind you of your true reality and identity. What are you? Who are you? Since you are the child of the *Supreme Consciousness*, you are divine just as I am. There is no difference between you and Me. The only difference is that I know I am Divine, but you do not. My purpose is therefore to bring you back to the level of God-awareness. I want you to cultivate inner vision and strive to attain oneness with God. *"Ekathwam Brahmathwam"* - unity is consciousness. So, strive to attain this unity, this oneness with God. Then you will have immeasurable bliss and peace.

I shall tell you something to help you in your endeavour to achieve this awareness and attain the state of oneness. Do not think that you are human and that you have to raise yourself to the level of divinity. Instead, think that you are basically divine, that your intrinsic nature is divinity and that you are temporarily existing on the human plane, on the human level. It is better to think that you are divine and have become temporarily human than to think that you are human and have to become divine. The latter is an uphill task but the former attitude makes it easier. It is easier to regain something which you have lost rather than to create something new.

I'll give you an example to illustrate this. Assume that there is a teacher with a Ph.D. degree and that he is temporarily obliged to teach children at the primary school level. Imagine another teacher with an ordinary Bachelor's degree is asked to guide Ph.D. research scholars. The second teacher's task is naturally difficult and may be quite impossible. He impossible. He will find it difficult to raise himself to a higher standard or status. But the first is aware of his true worth and value and will easily regain his original standard or status.

Your first and foremost mission in life is to gain inner vision and to realize your inherent divinity. Just as a river finds its way back to the ocean, you have to find your way back to your Maker. This is the reason for which you have been born. This is the true purpose of life. Life is not mere existence, it means living meaningfully and usefully. When once you realize the true purpose of life, you will stop existing and start living. Animals and birds and other creatures "exist" but human beings should learn to "live". Therefore, develop inner vision and gain inner peace and happiness. Realize, experience and have bliss.

INNER STRENGTH - ATMA SHAKTI

Today, I shall tell you what Inner Strength is. People normally talk about having a strong heart, having a strong mind and being a strong person. When do you say that a person is "strong"? It is when he subjugates his mind to his intellect. When he is not swayed by the vagaries of his mind, when he is not influenced by the likes and dislikes of his mind, when his thoughts, words and actions are not sheared by the whims and fancies of his mind, then he is a strong person. When he follows his intellect and reasoning power, when he weighs every thought, word and action against the yardstick of discrimination, when he performs every action according to the judgement and dictates of the voice of intellect i.e., the conscience, then he is a strong person. A strong person is therefore one who follows his intellect and not his mind. And since his intellect is always rational, logical, unbiased and unprejudiced, he will do only what is right and proper.

Now, there is another type of strength in you, which is far more valuable and precious, which is infinite and limitless. And this strength is your Inner Strength, what is known as *Atma-Shakti* or *Atma-balam*. It is valuable and precious because it is divine; it is infinite and limitless because it is God. It is present in you like the unfathomable ocean. It's richness and resources, power and potential are vast, immeasurable and inexhaustible. It is there in you, waiting to be discovered, experienced and utilised.

How do you begin to discover and experience your Inner Strength? Who are you, really? You are God. The divine spark exists in you and in everyone and is only waiting to blaze forth into the fire of *Shakti*. You have to ignite the spark and set it ablaze. For this, you should develop inner vision. Turn inwards within yourself and search for your true identity. Inquire, discriminate, analyse and deduce. With the help of *vichaara* and *viveka*, pull down the veil of maya which clouds and obscures your inner vision. With the help of *dhyana* and *sadhana*, try to find your true self, recognise your true nature and realize your true relationship with God. Break down all the barriers between us. Think and feel and experience yourself as one with Me. Develop this feeling of oneness and unity with Me and discard for ever, all the feelings of separateness and difference. There is no difference. *Tat thwam ekoham.* You and I are one. When you realize this truth, you will begin to experience your *Atma Shakti*, your Inner Strength.

Once you discover Inner Strength, you will feel an unparalleled sense of bliss, peace and love. You will feel yourself growing and expanding and filled with love for the whole world. An unshakable ecstasy of bliss and peace will fill and pervade your spirit. In this state of God-awareness and oneness, you are able to find your happiness and joy within yourself and not without. You attain the state of sublime serenity where nothing and nobody can shake you, throw you, hurt you or upset you. You feel equal to meeting any challenge or crisis in your life; you feel capable of facing any catastrophe or calamity boldly and bravely. Your Inner Strength gives you a sense of supreme confidence and fearlessness.

This is your real strength - *Atma Shakti*. This is the truth. There is no problem or difficulty in the world which cannot be solved or overcome by this *Shakti* because its strength is vast, unlimited and infinite whereas everything pertaining to the physical world is small, limited and finite. *Atma Shakti* can reduce any material problem to nothing because the power of the spirit is infinitely greater than the power of matter.

Therefore, my dear, discover your own Inner Strength, experience your innate potential and realize your divine power.

YOU MAKE YOUR OWN DESTINY

How often you hear people say "I am fated to be unhappy" or "I am destined to suffer in this life". They talk so loosely and lightly about Fate and Destiny. But, do they even stop to think what exactly is meant by Fate and Destiny? Who makes Fate? Who shapes Destiny? Who decides Fortune? Is it some invisible judge or referee who makes calculations and charts out people's future? Is it some unseen power which metes out joys and sorrows, fortunes and misfortunes? What are the answers to all these questions?

Fate or Destiny is nothing but the direct product or result of *Karmic* Law. The Law of *Karma* states that for every action there is an equal and opposite reaction, resound and reflection. This means that the result obtained is directly proportionate to the action performed. If the action is good, the result will be good; if the action is bad the result will also be bad. To put it simply then, you reap only what you sow, no more and no less. Sometimes the result is obtained immediately, sometimes after a few years, sometimes in a succeeding birth. Hindu Philosophy calls this result the "fruit of action". The layman calls it Fate or Destiny.

You are the person who performs the action, who thinks, plans, decides and chooses to take a particular course of action. You are the one who sets the law of *Karma* in motion by your action. It is your action which causes the wheel to turn. So, it is only right to conclude that you yourself make your own destiny, and not some invisible judge or power or even God. Yes, even God has no hand in your destiny. He is only the Witness. The real maker is you. You are the maker of your destiny, you are the arbiter of your fate. The sooner everyone realizes this, the better it will be for him. For only then will they learn to be judicious and cautious in their actions.

The success or failure of your life depends upon you - upon your thinking and your intelligence. If you possess a strong mind and intellect, you are bound to meet with success. Everything depends upon your inner strength. In a garden, for example, you see many plants. Some plants grow up strong and sturdy and soon blossom and bear healthy fruits. Some others remain weak and vulnerable and soon wilt and fade away. So you see, the richness and worthiness of your life depend upon your inherent innate strength.

Some people blame life, circumstances, situations and all the others around them for any misfortune which may befall them. Too often you hear them lament, "He has spoilt my life" or "She has ruined my happiness." Statements and accusations like these stem mainly from ignorance. If you fail in an examination, will you blame the question paper, the teacher, the examiner or perhaps your pen? It is a ridiculous thought, is it not? You fail because you have not prepared well enough. No one is to blame but you. It is the same in the case of life also. There is no use in blaming circumstances or other people for your misfortunes or failures. Other people are only tools and instruments. They are only cogs in the wheel of fortune. But the one who operates the wheel is you yourself.

You can either make or mar your life. The future depends upon you, destiny lies in your hands. So, be careful in what you think, say and do. Sathyam vada, dharmam chara. Speak the truth and walk in righteousness. This is the secret formula for success. No matter what the odds are, have the determination to succeed and you will. If you have strength of will and discipline, you can do anything. You will be the captain of your ship and the master of your destiny.

FREE WILL Vs DESTINY

There are many arguments and discussions about Free Will and Destiny. People talk of Free Will as one thing and of Destiny as another. They treat them as two totally different concepts and theories. They could not be more wrong about this.

I have already told you that you make your own destiny and carve your own fate. Your future is shaped by you and you alone, by your motives, your impulses, your desires, your thoughts and your actions. What is Free Will, after all? It is the free thinking power given to you by God. It is this power which helps you to reason and rationalise, analyse and adjudge, discriminate and decide. It is this power which moves you to thought, word and action.

As I have said before, destiny is the result or fruit of your action. Action stems from your free will. Therefore, destiny is the direct consequence of your free will. When the action is performed, the result is automatically destined. In other words, free will is the cause and destiny is the effect. So you see, Free Will and Destiny are not two different things. They are closely interwoven, inter-linked and inter-related. Free Will shapes your destiny and destiny depends upon your free will.

Some people say, "I am destined to suffer in this life" as if some unseen power is responsible for apportioning happiness and unhappiness. They do not realize that they are reaping the consequences of their own actions. The suffering they have to undergo in the present life is the effect of some misdeeds performed out of their own free will in some previous birth. Sometimes you may think, "I have not done anything wrong or harmed anyone in my life, then why should this catastrophe befall me?" Yes, you may not have done anything wrong or harmed... anyone in this, your present life. But, you most certainly must have done something wrong and improper in your previous life for which you have to pay the penalty now. Remember, all *Karmic* debts have to be cancelled, all penalties have to be paid. This is the law of *Karma* and no one can be exempted from it. You do not realize this principle because you do not remember your past lives. If you remember them, then acceptance will be easy and your suffering will be mitigated. Therefore, to think and say that your destiny is determined by some great invisible power or force is sheer ignorance. It is better that you realize straight away that it is your own free will which is responsible for your destiny, in this birth and in the next.

What do you learn from this? You learn that your fortune or misfortune is entirely dependent upon your free will. It is your free will which shapes the course of your destiny. I'll give you an example to illustrate this point. Suppose there are two persons A and B. A is a wise, careful person, a good thinker and planner; B, on the other hand, is a foolish and careless person, a spendthrift and wastrel. Assume that both A and B are given a certain amount of money and told to utilise it as they think fit. Remember, both receive the same amount of money. A, being the type of person he is, makes judicious investments and succeeds in getting good returns on his capital. But B, being the type of person he is, indulges in senseless speculation and wastes away all his capital carelessly. Here, you have two persons who possess the same commodity, but the ways in which they use it are diametrically opposite, because their thinking is entirely different from each other's. One gains abundantly while the other loses colossally.

It is the same in the case of life also. Each one of you has been given the same free will with the same reasoning and discriminating power. You can use it either to your advantage or disadvantage, for your betterment or detriment. Your free will decides the course of your actions and determines the result of your actions. Your free will decides the future events in your life and the joys and sorrows to come.

Therefore, my dear, give up the delusion that destiny is ordained by the Gods. It is not so. Your destiny is ordained by your free will alone, and the sooner you realize this, the better it will be for you. At least from now, try to create a good destiny for yourself by engaging in good works and deeds. You cannot undo the past and the present has to be borne. But you can certainly make a good future by engaging yourself in good actions now. Forget the past, bear with the present and work for the future.

DHARMA - I
(SWADHARMA IS ATMA - DHARMA)

Divyatma Swaroopa! What is *dharma*? What does the word "*dharma*" mean? Does it refer merely to religion and righteousness? No, for it also means duty and code of conduct. When God created man, He endowed him with an intellect and the power to think and reason for himself. As society grew and developed, man evolved and established certain codes of conduct and laws of living. They were absolutely necessary for preserving and maintaining morality and righteousness. These codes and laws have become *manava dharma* - devised by man for the use of man. Thus *manava dharma* is actually a yardstick of good behaviour, conduct and morality. It is only when there is a yardstick of comparison that man will be able to recognise what is right and wrong, proper and improper, moral and immoral. So *dharma* is a kind of measuring rod against which man tests his conduct, thoughts, emotions, desires, values and actions. *Dharma* enables him to think, analyse and decide what is the right and proper thing to do. Without *dharma*, there can be no *karma*. *Dharma* decides and determines *karma*.

Now, when you look at a person's life from childhood to adulthood, you see that the same person takes on different roles at different points of time. And the

76

dharma too differs according to the role being played at that time. Thus, as a child its duty and obligation i.e., its dharma is to be an obedient child, a good and diligent student etc. When the child grows up and attains adulthood, his *dharma* changes. As a man, he begins to earn his livelihood and look after his family. His *dharma* is to be a good provider and supporter, look after the needs of his family with love and affection and do this work honestly, sincerely and earnestly. This is *purusha dharma.*

As a woman, the *dharma* is to be a good wife, mother and daughter-in-law and to care for her husband, children and in-laws with love, understanding, compassion and tolerance. This is *Stree dharma.*

The parents' *dharma* is to bring up their children according to good standards and to instil in them high principles of thinking and living. Once the children grow up and their affairs are settled, the parents' worldly responsibilities are over. This, according to Indian custom is the time of *Sashti poorthi.* "*Sashti*" means responsibilities and "*poorthi*" means fulfilment. Once the worldly responsibilities are fulfilled, the husband and wife set out together on the spiritual path. They turn their minds towards God and adopt a life of *sadhana*. This is the real meaning of sashti poorthi. Nowadays, as soon as people attain sixty years of age, they perform their *sashti poorthi* blindly, as a conventional ritual, without knowing the true significance. They perform the ceremony and immediately resume their worldly ways. Thus, you find that in one person's life, there are so many different *dharmas*.

Manava dharma was conceived and prescribed by our ancient sages for two reasons. One reason was that *dharma* is necessary to maintain morality in society. Norms of discipline and codes of conduct are essential to preserve integrity and humanity. The second reason was that *dharma* is a way to God. *Dharma* is righteousness and righteousness is God. So *dharma* leads you to God. When you live according to your *dharma*, sincerely and earnestly, you lead a Godly life and you automatically grow closer to God. Even an atheist is close to God when he practises his *dharma* single-pointedly and unswervingly. The various *dharmas*, therefore, are stepping-stones to God.

While manava *dharma* was devised by man, there is another *dharma* which is much more important and significant. This is the only dharma laid down by God Himself, the only *dharma* which He revealed through the *Vedas* and the *Upanishads*. This is the highest and most exalted *dharma* - *Madhava dharma* - and is also your *swadharma*. "Swa" means self or one's own. So *Swadharma* is one's own *dharma* or the *dharma* which one owes to oneself. This *Swadharma* is *Atma-dharma* and it refers to your duty or obligation to realize that you are the *Atma*, that you are Divine. Therefore *Atma-jnana* is *Atma-dharma*.

You owe your very existence to God. You came from Him, you live in Him and you go back to Him. He created you and gave you life-breath. It is He who is with you continuously through all your births and life-times, not your parents, friends, brothers or sisters. Therefore, you owe your allegiance first to Him. Your first and foremost obligation is towards Him, to recognise your relationship to Him and to realize that you and He are one. This is the highest *dharma* of man and is one that is the most natural as befits his human status. *Atma-jnana* is your birthright. You have to work your way towards this knowledge and realization. *Atma-dharma* is your inherent and intrinsic *dharma* and it surpasses all other worldly dharmas. I shall tell you more about it tomorrow.

DHARMA - II
(GIVE UP ALL DHARMAS)

Yesterday, I told you about the superiority of *Atma-dharma* over other *dharmas*. The first is God-given and the second man-given. Having been born as a human being, it is your primary duty to recognise your *Atma-dharma* and to pursue it. However, pursuing your *Atma-dharma* is not an easy task. The material world places many constrictions on you, and you yourself are bound by various responsibilities, obligations and commitments. You are hemmed in by innumerable restrictions, rules and regulations. In the face of all these obstacles, how are you to follow your *Atma-dharma* with single-pointed concentration? The answer to this is contained in the *Gita*. The *Gita* lays down very clearly and precisely how you should act and behave with respect to your *Atma-dharma*.

Before dealing with *dharma*, let us examine the *karma* aspect. First of all, the *Gita* says :-

"Karmanyeva adhikaraste ma phaleshu kadachana"

What does this line mean? It simply means that you should perform all actions without having an eye on the fruits or rewards thereof. Your actions should be dictated by your *dharma* and not by the fruits that are likely to result in.

The *Gita* then goes on to say - *"Mayee sarvaani karmaani"* - surrender all actions to Me. Surrendering your actions to God means that whatever act or deed you undertake is done for His sake, for His pleasure and for His approval. You offer every act at His Feet just as you would offer a flower or a fruit. Thus every act of yours becomes a `naivedhya' (offering). When you thus surrender your actions to God, you will naturally and automatically surrender the fruits of the actions also to Him. You will not look for any reward or return. The act is His and the fruit also is His. In this way, you renounce your right over the fruits - *Karma phala thyaga*. Your only desire is to perform Easwareeya *karma*, the Lord's work; you have no desire for benefits.

Now, which part of your self is it that is associated with impulses, motives, desires, etc. ? It is the mind. It is the mind which craves, the mind which covets, the mind which desires. So, when the *Gita* exhorts you to relinquish your desire for the fruits of action, it is actually the mind which has to renounce and relinquish. You cannot surrender the act and the fruit without surrendering your mind. Therefore, when you talk of *"karma phala thyaga"*, it actually means the surrender of the mind to God.

And now, let us take up the question of *dharma*. Towards the end, the *Gita* says :-

81

"*Sarva dharmaan parithyajya*" - (Give up all *dharmas* to Me).

What does this statement mean? Some people think that giving up all *dharmas* means giving up all duties and actions and so they take refuge in inaction. But this is not the true explanation. Nowhere in the *Gita* is it said that you should stop performing action. No one can desist from *karma*. As long as the world exists, *karma* has to be performed. You cannot avoid it or escape it. Then, what does giving up *dharmas* really mean? I shall explain it to you.

Yesterday, I told you how *manava dharma* evolved. It was the human intellect which devised and established codes, norms, standards, doctrines, rules, regulations etc., all of which collectively form *dharma*. It is therefore the intellect which reasons and decides what is *dharma* and what is *adharma*. Anything which follows the prescribed pattern is *dharma* and anything which goes against it is *adharma*. It is the intellect which has to measure and weigh each action against the yardstick of *dharma* and eventually decide what is right and what is wrong, what is moral and what is immoral and so on.

Sometimes, you are filled with doubts and dilemmas as to what is proper *dharma* and what is not. Is a certain course of action *dharmic* or *adharmic*?

82

Is this decision or that option *dharmic* or *adharmic*? This sort of uncertainty leads to a lot of confusion and unrest. And this is where the statement "*sarva dharmaan parithyajya*" comes into play. It means that you should give up all your notions of *dharma* and *adharma* to God. Leave it to Him to decide what is right and what is wrong, what is proper and what is improper, what is *dharma* and what is *adharma*. This means that you have to surrender your sense of judgement and reasoning to God. Which part of your self reasons and analyses? It is the intellect. So, giving up your *dharmas* to God actually amounts to surrendering your intellect to Him. This means that you have to give up the right to resolve or refuse, decide or dispute, accept or reject, omit or commit, plan or plot. In short, you say, "O' Lord, I cannot think and decide for myself any more. You think and decide for me. Whatever You decide will be my law, whatever You will shall be my command." In this way, you surrender your intellect completely to Him and leave it to Him to decide what is appropriate and what is not. Whatever He decides for you, you accept willingly and cheerfully; wherever He places you, you are blissful and serene. Your only desire is to carry out His Will, to serve Him and to please Him.

This, then, is the true explanation of the statement "surrender all *dharmas* to Me". First, you surrender your mind, then you surrender your intellect.

Once these two barriers are transcended, you will reach Him quickly and swiftly. Your only *dharma* will be your *Atma-dharma*, your only desire will be for Him, for liberation and merging. But in time, this desire also will fade away. You surrender even your desire for liberation to Him. "Let Him liberate me when He wishes. It is enough for me that I fill myself with love for Him." - this is what your attitude will be.

STREE DHARMA

Very little is said about *Stree dharma* nowadays. In fact, people are quite ignorant as to what it actually means. Some confuse stree *dharma* with stree *karma*, not knowing that the two of them are quite different from each other. Today I'll tell you what exactly is meant by *Stree dharma*.

There are two meanings to the word *"dharma"*. One meaning is code of conduct and behaviour. I have already told you that *dharma* was laid down by man himself as a guideline and yardstick of goodness and righteousness. *Dharma* also determines *karma*. Rules, regulations and requisites which collectively form *dharma* also prescribe the right deed and the right action. For example, the *dharma* of a soldier is to protect his motherland, so his *karma* is to fight. The *dharma* of a teacher is to impart education and knowledge, so his *karma* is to teach through lessons and precepts. Therefore, first is *dharma*, next comes *karma*.

When you talk about stree *dharma* in the context of conduct and behaviour, it is quite clear what it requires. The *dharma* of a woman is to be a good daughter and later to be a good daughter-in-law, wife and mother. According to this *dharma*, her *karma* dictates that she should study well and gain a good education. When she marries, she should serve her in-laws and husband lovingly. She has to look after her children and their needs and pay proper attention to their upbringing. She has to manage the household and keep it running smoothly and efficiently. She should discharge all her duties with love, affection, patience, tolerance, compassion, understanding, sympathy, gentleness, kindness and above all, with humility. All this is declared in our *Shastras* and scriptures and is known to people.

But there is another aspect of stree *dharma* which has been obscured over the past years and been forgotten and which I shall now bring to light. What does the word "*dharma*" really mean? It means nature or quality or attribute - "*guna*". For example, the nature of fire is to scorch and burn and give out warmth and light. This is its *dharma* or *guna*. The attribute of the wind is to blow - this is its *dharma* or *guna*. Without the particular attribute or quality, fire will not be fire and wind will not be wind.

In the context of *dharma* meaning *guna*, what then is Stree *dharma*? The word "*stree*" has three syllables - SA, TA and RA. SA is "*Swabhimaanam*" (self-respect); TA is "*thyagam*" (sacrifice) and RA is "*rasa*" (sweetness). These are the three basic and inherent qualities of a woman. Without them, a woman is no woman at all. Of the three *gunas*, *swabhimaanam* or self-respect is the most important for a woman. Without self-respect, a woman cannot live happily and peacefully. If she loses her self-respect and dignity, she falls in her own estimation and value and is unable to live a serene life. For instance, *Draupadi* was stripped of her dignity in the court of *Dhritarashtra* and this cruel and ignoble offense lowered her image in her own eyes and caused her to lose her self-respect. That is why she became so vengeful towards the *Kauravas* and incited the *Pandava* brothers against them. Hence, it is not only harmful but sometimes even dangerous for a woman to lose her self-respect.

Self-respect is like a vesture to a woman; chastity and virtue are her ornaments. So it is the first and foremost duty of every woman to protect and preserve her dignity and self-respect. She should not go anywhere or do anything which may endanger her self-respect and injure her dignity. Her primary obligation is to retain and maintain her self-respect. Of course, if she has children, then she should place their welfare and interests first, before her own.

So, remember this, my dear. Never lose your self-respect, otherwise you will find it difficult to live with yourself. If you suffer loss of dignity at the hands of someone else, you will be left with feelings of anger, hate and resentment. If you suffer loss of dignity through your own action, you will be left with feelings of shame and guilt and you will not be able to forgive yourself for your misdeed. Either way, life becomes difficult and uncomfortable. Therefore, a woman should always safeguard her self-respect and dignity jealously, zealously and righteously. This is her right, this is her due, this is what she owes to herself. Self-respect is to a woman what fragrance is to a flower and sweetness is to sugar. Without fragrance and sweetness what remains?

THE FINAL SURRENDER

I have told you so far how you surrender first your desire and mind, and then your intellect and reasoning. At a higher stage of surrender, you transcend all *dharmas* and realize that *Atma-dharma* is the only really important dharma in your life. When you talk about *navavidha bhakti* (the nine types of *bhakti*), you say that *atma-nivedanam* is the ultimate stage in the path of devotion. But let me tell you that *atma-nivedanam* is actually not the ultimate stage. There is one more stage after this and that is *atma-arpanam*. *Atma-arpanam* is the final surrender, the last step that leads to self-realization and God-consciousness. I shall now explain to you the difference between *atma-nivedanam* and *atma-arpanam*.

What is "*nivedana*"? What does this word actually mean? It means "*prayer*", so *atma-nivedanam* is a prayer, or plea or request to God to accept your offering of your self. Now, when you pray to God for something, you normally look for a response from Him. You want an acknowledgment from Him and an answer to your prayer or request. You may think that you have no such wish or want, but it does exist. Even without your conscious knowledge, you will be looking for a response and acknowledgment from Him. So, this little feeling or desire is left in you, even after you think you have done *atma-nivedanam*.

89

But *atma-arpanam* goes a step higher. "*Arpan*" means offering and *atma-arpanam* denotes a complete surrender or giving up of your self, without any desire on your part for a response or acknowledgment from God. It is unconditional surrender. In this stage, you give up all your desires and feelings, even your desire for liberation and merging. You are in a state of absolute desirelessness. The only feeling left in you is supreme love and attachment for your Lord. It is now that you become hollow, like a reed or a pipe. You are like the "*murali*" or "*bansuri*" (flute) in the Hands of the Lord. He plays with you, breathes through you, lives through you, acts through you and works through you. You become inseparable from God and a part of Him. You are like *Krishna's* flute, the instrument through which He produces the divine melody of love, sweetness and oneness.

I'll give you some examples to explain the difference better. *Atma-nivedanam* is like sending a registered parcel to someone with an acknowledgment due form attached to it. The receiver has to sign and send back the acknowledgment due form, for which you are waiting eagerly. Has my parcel reached him, you wonder. Did I write the address correctly? When will I receive the acknowledgment? Will he sign the form himself or let someone else do it? All these and other questions, doubts, uncertainties and feelings will be taking hold of you. You are impatient until you receive the acknowledgment.

90

On the other hand, *atma-arpanam* is like depositing the parcel quietly on the door step of the person's house, without mentioning your name and address. The receiver has no way of sending you a receipt of acknowledgment. But you are not bothered by any doubts or questions. You take it for granted that your parcel has reached its destination and you are serenely content in your certainty and knowledge. You have no desire or even curiosity about an acknowledgment. You have no feeling in you or thought clamouring for a response or reciprocation.

Atma-nivedanam is like *Sathyabhama*. *Sathyabhama* loved *Krishna*, no doubt, and served Him fully and with great love and devotion. But she was always wanting His approval and seeking His appreciation. She always wanted *Krishna* to acknowledge her love for Him. So, there was a little bit of rajas in her *bhakti*.

Whereas, *atma-arpanam* is like *Rukmini*. *Rukmini* also loved and served *Krishna* with all her heart and mind. And her devotion was absolutely selfless and unselfish. She never sought any acknowledgment, approval or appreciation from her Lord. It was enough for her that she was able to love Him and serve Him. She was completely *sathwic*, with not an ounce of *rajas* or *tamas* in her.

So you see, my dear, what a fine distinction there is between *atma-nivedanam* and *atma-arpanam*. *Atma-arpanam* is the final and ultimate state in the *bhakti marga* (path of devotion). *Atma-nivedanam* gives you a feeling of happiness, joy and ecstasy. *Atma-arpanam* gives you a sense of unequalled bliss and peace. *Atma-nivedanam* is *paraa-bhakti* (devotion which is beyond ordinary knowledge and comprehension). *Atma-arpanam* is *apoorva-bhakti* (devotion which is unequalled and unparalleled, the highest devotion).

And what of the Lord? What is His response when a devotee has performed *atma-arpanam*? By such an act, the Lord is completely bound by the devotee in golden fetters. He becomes the slave of His devotee and is duty-bound to look after him and care for him at every step. He guides the foot-steps of his devotee even as the mother guides the foot-steps of her infant who is just learning to walk. Thus the Lord is constantly by the devotee's side, guiding, guarding and helping him to walk along the path of *samsara* until, eventually, the devotee reaches the Gates of Heaven and takes the last few steps towards the eternal *Sannidhi* of the Divine Lord.

What greater devotion can there be than this? What greater bliss? What greater peace?

ALTER YOUR ATTITUDE

So many things happen in the world which are beyond your control. Misfortunes, losses, disappointments, tragedies, bereavements-all these and more. And then there are the petty little irritations and annoyances, frictions and disturbances, worries and anxieties which weigh you down and cause you to be upset. Sometimes, you are so worn down by cares that you wonder if life is worth living at all. I don't say that it is wrong to have such a feeling or that it is not proper to have such a thought. No, it is quite a natural feeling which arises from a particular state of mind.

But, just sit back and ponder for a while on the lives of some of the greatest saints who ever walked the earth-Socrates, Moses, Kabir, Ramdas, Meerabai, Ramana Maharshi and many more like them. If you think deeply, you will realize that all of them had one thing in common apart from their faith, and that is suffering. All of them knew and experienced suffering in some form or another, be it poverty, sickness, personal loss, harassment or some other hardship. In fact, they had to face all the kinds of troubles which befall an ordinary human being and perhaps more so in extent and degree. These people were not angels in disguise or super human beings. They were ordinary people with ordinary bodies like anyone else, with the same God-given mind and intellect.

93

Have these people been known to have raved against their fate or complained bitterly about their strait? Did they ever allow a trial or a tribulation to affect their state of exaltation? Just think about them for a minute. What is it that lifted them out of the ordinary and made them into saints? What is it that gave them the hall-mark of great persons and enlightened souls? The answer is quite simple. It was their state of mind which turned them into superior beings. They had a mental attitude and a certain outlook which raised them from the level of mediocrity and lifted them to sainthood.

Yes, my dear, the only difference between you and them is your state of mind. Remove this difference and you will also become a saint. As I said earlier, there are so many uncontrollable factors in your life. Something may happen which affects you deeply. You cannot change it as it is beyond your ability. But, there is one thing which you can change, which is within your ability, and that is your own attitude. Change your attitude if not the situation; change your outlook if not the circumstance. If you can do this, you will have neither pain nor suffering.

You will now ask Me-how should I change my attitude and outlook? I'll tell you this also. First of all, give up self-pity. You should not feel sorry for yourself if life deals you a blow or if you do not get what you want. Self-pity is self destruction. It is the root cause of all discontent, and leads to depression, despondency and despair. Self-pity stems from selfishness and self-centredness. If you keep on thinking in terms of "*I*" and "*Mine*", you can never get rid of self-pity. God first, others next, I last-this should be your attitude. There is a lot of joy and satisfaction when you cultivate this attitude and apply it in practical life.

Secondly, learn to live for others and not for yourself. The greatest joy lies in making others happy. The greatest happiness lies in comforting the distressed and consoling the disappointed. The greatest satisfaction lies in alleviating the pain, suffering and misery of another.

Thirdly, learn to accept bravely and cheerfully whatever life has to offer you-pains or gains, bumps or jumps. Life is the best teacher, use its lessons as foot-holds in the ladder of progress. Climb the ladder and emerge a strong and wise person

If you try to practise these three things in life, you will find living much easier, more satisfying and most worthwhile.

WHAT IS DEATH ?

Most of you weep and wail, mourn and bemoan when your loved one is separated from you by death. You feel bereaved and bereft, lost and lonely because of the absence of your loved one from your side. But such feelings arise out of foolishness, illusion and delusion - *Maya*. For, this death is no real death at all. It is only a transition from one state to another, from one level to another. Just as you graduate from childhood to adolescence and then to adulthood, death is a graduation from the physical world of matter to the ethereal world of the spirit. With death, one sheds the coils of the mortal world, the whirlpool of *Samsara* and steps into the real, immortal world where love and service are the only bonds, the only attachments. Yes, the world of ether and the astral worlds are the reality, for that is where pure consciousness exists without the veil of *Maya*. This objective world of desires, of wants and pleasures, of sensual delights and enjoyments is not the reality.

This world is only a temporary, transient traveller's route. You are all fellow travellers coming in and out of the great big travellers' bungalow. Some of you leave early, some others leave later. But all of you have to leave at some time because this is not your final destination. You have to go on to the next world.

There is a saying in English - *"While in Rome do as the Romans do"*. As long as you are in the physical world, you need your physical body. You cannot live in this world without a body. A physical body is necessary as a vehicle to travel through this world. But when the time comes for you to graduate to the higher world, you leave your physical body behind and don your astral one. You need an astral body to live in the astral world. You cannot live in the physical world with an astral body nor can you live in the astral world with a physical body. This is a natural law. Your physical body is like a ticket of entry. When you make your exit, you discard it.

So, my dear, why do you think of death as separation? It is not separation, it is transition and graduation. If your loved one graduates before you do, why do you weep? Is it not foolish and even selfish? Instead, you should rejoice and exult that he or she has gained the graduation certificate. Learn from the graduates. Take a lesson from their good deeds. And if they have committed mistakes, learn from them also. Every experience, good or bad, whether yours or someone else's is a valuable lesson. Experience is education. Whether you benefit from it or not, it is up to you.

What, then, is real death? If shedding the physical body is not death, what else is? I shall tell you.

Death is destruction of desires and of the ego. Subduing your ego, reducing your worldly desires, cutting your attachments - all this is real death. A man without desires is the most contented of all. He is also the happiest and the most tranquil. Therefore, in order to progress and evolve, it is necessary to first cut down desires. I am not telling you to take an axe to your desires at once. It is impossible to get rid of desires at one stroke. But you can start by laying a ceiling on your desires. Keep your desires within limits. Learn to make do with what you have. Don't desire what is beyond your reach. I shall tell you more about this later.

CEILING ON DESIRES

What is ceiling? Ceiling means limit. Ceiling on desires means placing a limit on desires. It does not mean cutting off all desires or putting an end to them. This is not possible, for as long as man exists, desires will exist. Man is human because he has desires. Without desires, he becomes divine. And this is a state which cannot be acquired very easily. But at least, you can make a start by limiting your desires and by placing a curb on them.

What exactly does the term *"ceiling on desires"* mean? You know that human beings have manifold desires and wants-material, worldly, physical, social etc. Some of these are within your reach but some of them are not. For example, it is common for a rich man to possess a tape-recorder, a refrigerator, a V.C.R. etc. But is it possible for a poor man living in a hut to possess them? Such possessions are well out of his reach and he will never be able to obtain them. It is, therefore, useless to even aspire for such possessions. Any such hankerings and longings will only lead to despair, frustration and unrest.

There is a proverb in English - *"Cut your coat according to your cloth"*. Properly translated into life, it means that you have to regulate and restrict your needs and wants according to the resources available to you. You have to learn to fashion your life, your living, your social status, your luxuries, your comforts etc., according to your own affordability and capability. If you apply this principle to your daily living, you will find that your life becomes more pleasant and much easier. You will realize that it is absurd and useless to desire what is beyond your reach and ability. Learn this first. Learn to desire only what you can have and not what you cannot. You have to train your mind very judiciously in this matter. Whenever you find a desire rising up in your mind, weigh it carefully. Is it right for me to harbour such a desire? Shall I be able to obtain the object of my desire? Or is it outside the limits of practicality? Am I clamouring for the moon or reaching for the stars? These are the questions you should ask yourself.

In this regard, you should remember one thing always. Your intellect will tell you what is right and what is wrong. Whenever the mind comes up with any want, wish, need or desire, put up a petition to your intellect and request it to weigh all the pros and cons of the issue. The intellect will never give you wrong advice because it is rational, logical and discriminating. It is the mind which is swayed this way and that by various factors. It is the mind which leads you down dark alleys, wrong paths and by-lanes. But the intellect always keeps to the straight and true path. Therefore, follow the directions of the intellect and you will never tread the wrong road.

Whenever you find an unreasonable desire taking hold of your mind, you have to ruthlessly discard it. If you find it difficult to do this, then you should try to trim it down to suit your limitations.

History is full of incidents and stories about men who were defeated by their own ends. Kamsa, Ravana, Duryodhana, Alexander, Napoleon, Hitler-all of them are examples of human beings who were destroyed by their own over reaching ambitions and desires. Desires, if not controlled, regulated and disciplined, will lead to your own downfall and destruction.

That is why I always tell you that you should learn to curb your desires. It is not wrong to desire what is within your means and power. But, when your desires begin to transcend the limits, they get out of hand and then the danger sets in. Therefore, my dear, start by laying a ceiling on your needs, wants and desires. Human beings have an amazing sense of adaptability and adjustment. A person can live luxuriously in a palace but can also learn to accommodate himself in a hovel, if need be. Don't you all give up your physical needs and comforts and live in Spartan-like simplicity when you go to *Prasanthi Nilayam*? It is only a matter of self-discipline and self-control. Self-control will lead to self-confidence, and self-confidence will lead to self-realization.

BE BOLD AND BEAUTIFUL

Boldness comes from self-confidence and beauty comes from inner peace.

You must learn to go through life boldly and bravely. Boldness is a result of self-confidence. Self-confidence springs from faith in yourself and in God. Whatever may be the odds, vicissitudes or trials in life, you must be confident that God will help you to face them. If you show just one ounce of determination, I shall give you a ton of strength. If you show one ounce of strength, I shall give you a ton of confidence. Remember, if you take just one step towards Me, I shall take ten steps towards you. Why ten, even hundred, if need be.

You should have the courage of your convictions. You should be able to stand up fearlessly for what you think is right. You should always fight for integrity, honesty, truth, righteousness and morality. These virtues are sadly on the decline nowadays. Therefore, it is very important to defend and protect them. I want every one of My devotees to fight for these virtues, bravely and boldly. It will not be an easy task. There will be storms and hurricanes. You will have to weather the storms and withstand the hurricanes. There can be no room for doubt, hesitation, uncertainty, timidity and weakness. Do not be afraid. Why should you have any fear or trepidation when you are in the right? It is like the *Mahabharata* war when the *Pandavas* defeated the *Kauravas* because they had justice on their side. The *Pandavas* had right, the *Kauravas* had might. And remember that I am always on the side of the right. As long as you have righteousness on your side, you have nought to fear. Step forth courageously and indomitably into the world's arena; face your enemies fearlessly and boldly; fight gallantly and sincerely for what you believe is the truth; you will then finish victoriously and also earn My Blessings.

Be beautiful by nature and spirit. True beauty lies in being pure of character and virtue. A virtuous person will always be loving, gentle and soft at heart. Cultivate purity of character and harmony of thought, word and action. Be tolerant, generous, helpful, forgiving, charitable, considerate and thoughtful towards all. Then, you will be a sincere *Sadhaka*, very dear to My heart. You will earn the boon of peace and bliss from Me.

The eyes are the mirror of the soul. Your face reflects the nature of your inner self. When your inner self is at peace and you are able to feel the bliss of the soul, the radiance of this sublime peace and bliss will be reflected in your eyes and on your face. The intrinsic purity of *Atma* is seen in the softness of your speech, the nobility of your manner and the gentleness of your disposition. This is true beauty, not regularity of features or proportion of form. Spiritual beauty is real beauty, and lasts for all eternity. It casts a glow of radiance and inno- cence over the face and an aura of tranquillity and restfulness around the person. This is the beauty that I would like to see in all My devotees.

Boldness and beauty of the spirit are the hall- marks of a true devotee. They are like identification marks. But unlike birth marks, these marks have to be cultivated, nurtured and fostered. So, try to attain these hall-marks through sincere effort and steadfast *Sadhana*.

THE POWER OF SILENCE

Silence is the nature of *Atma*. It is the language of the soul. It is through silence that the Voice of God can be heard; it is through silence that the Word of God can be understood.

Therefore, my dear, it is very important that you should learn to cultivate the art of silence. Inner silence or *Antar Mouna* is a very powerful state of being when the inner spirit or the inner self is able to manifest itself. What is this inner spirit or inner self? It is nothing but God, the Supreme Consciousness. Silence is the medium through which God manifests Himself and makes His Presence felt. Silence is the language of communication between you and your God. It is through silence that you can experience God.

Regarding the subject of silence, there are two things that I want to tell you. The first is about the state of silence. Now, silence can be either negative or positive. A silence which is filled with wasteful, useless thoughts is negative. An angry silence, a sulky silence, a brooding silence, a vengeful silence-all these are negative. They cause more harm than good and are detrimental to your mental state. On the other hand, a positive silence is one that is filled with good, noble and kindly thoughts. Such a silence is definitely beneficial to your mind.

The most beneficial silence is one that is filled with thoughts of the Divine. This is a state of silence which we, more generally, call the state of meditation or contemplation. Silent meditation or contemplation on God, if practised even for five or ten minutes every day will give you untold peace and tranquillity. This happens because all the senses are quiet and at rest when you are in a state of meditation. When all the senses are at rest, the mind also becomes calm and still. It is always the mind which is the centre of disquiet. So when the mind is calm, you have a feeling of peace and serenity.

This brings Me to the second point, namely continuing the silence for a while after you conclude your meditation. This is a very important rule to be observed. I'll tell you why. When you are in silent meditation, waves of peace are generated which slowly spread and vibrate through your entire system. It takes some time for the mind and the heart to absorb, retain and digest these vibrations. If you break your silence, these waves and vibrations will be dispersed and will go back to the source from which they came-the inner self or God. On the other hand, if you continue the act of silence, you will give the mind and heart time to absorb the vibrations.

You may ask - why is it necessary for the heart and mind to absorb the vibrations? The answer is quite simple. The purpose of meditation is first to purify the mind and the heart, so that you can reach God. The mind is always swayed by desires and the heart is torn by emotions. These two truant and errant organs have to be quietened and calmed. Silent meditation is the best way of doing this. Meditation is food for the mind just as *Bhojan* is sustenance for the body. And, silence is necessary for assimilation of the food by the mind just as physical rest is necessary immediately after taking a meal. Don't the doctors advise you to sit up for half an hour after a meal so as to facilitate digestion? Similarly, silence is necessary for the mind and heart to assimilate the peace vibrations which are set off during meditation.

Silence is the power of the spirit. If practised properly, it decreases the negative vibrations created by wasteful thinking and creates positive vibrations which are more beneficial to you. Practised over the years, silence helps the mind to achieve a state of peacefulness and detachment. This will improve your power of concentration. Out of this come better discrimination and better judgement. You will be able to think, speak and act more efficiently.

Therefore, my dear, realize the power of silence and learn to practise it at least for an hour every day soon after your meditation. The effect of silence is unseen and invisible but is tremendously powerful and beneficial.

RELIGION AND SPIRITUALITY

Some people confuse religion with spirituality. Some others think that religion is the same as spirituality. But let Me tell you this-they are not the same. They are quite different things though they are closely related.

What is meant by religion? Religion is the way to God. It is a collective system of beliefs, rites, rituals, practices and prayers which propitiate God and lead you closer to Him. A person who is religious is a holy and devout person, no doubt. He can be called a devotee and an ardent worshipper of his particular chosen God. But, a religious person tends to keep his belief and faith away from his everyday life. His devotion, prayers and *Pooja* are kept strictly within the four walls of his *Pooja* room. His devotion and his God are not allowed to mix with the rest of his life. Sometimes, he is one person in the *Pooja* room and a totally different person outside it. I know of people who sit for hours in the *Pooja* room reading the *Namavali* or chanting *Slokas*, then come out and start scolding and abusing the servant for some mistake committed. Then, there are those who observe the rituals of *Pooja* and the auspicious days of worship, meticulously and unfailingly, but yet indulge in scandal mongering, frivolous gossip, selfishness and meanness. Of course, I do not say that all religious people are like this.

What I am merely trying to say is that they tend to keep religion away from life. To them, the two are different and have to be kept apart. I don't say that it is wrong. But it is an immature attitude.

What, on the other hand, is spirituality? Spirituality is the science of the *Atma*. What is *Atma*? It is love, it is truth, it is peace, it is bliss, it is joy. It is *Sathchithananda*. A person who believes that he is *Atma* or *Satchithananda* and tries to live and behave in a way which befits his natural, divine self is, in fact, a spiritual person. Knowing his divine nature, he tries to apply his knowledge into everyday life by practising love, tolerance, sympathy, compassion, goodwill, equanimity, etc. Loving His God, he tries to transform his life from a human to a divine one. Such a person is not just a spiritual person or merely a devotee but he can be called a true disciple of God.

So you see, my dear, there is a vast difference between religion and spirituality, between a religious person and a spiritual person. At the same time, you cannot say that the two are completely distinct and different. No, this is not so at all. Although different, they are closely linked, just as the child is linked to its mother. Religion is the child, and spirituality is the adult. Devotion in the initial budding, growing and developmental stage is religion. Once fully developed, advanced and matured, it is spirituality.

109

You can say that religion is more of theoretical knowledge while spirituality is its practical application. Thus religion, when applied to life and practised actively and diligently, becomes spirituality. A person who applies his religious beliefs, principles and doctrines to his practical life and tries to live according to these standards, is no longer just a religious being but a spiritual being. The devotee becomes a disciple, a true aspirant of Truth and seeker of God. This is the way it should be. Thus, religion is a view of life while spirituality is a way of life. One seeks to know Divinity, the other seeks to experience it. One strives for God, the other lives in God. Religion shows the way to God, spirituality treads the path to God.

PRACTISE MY PRESENCE

The ultimate goal of every *Bhaktha* is to reach the Divine *Sannidhi* or the Divine shelter of the Lord. This Divine shelter or Refuge does not exist in some far-off place but is there in your own mind and in your own heart. The Lord is present in you. He is there, so close to you, at your very beck and call. But do you know how to reach out to Him? Do you know how to summon Him? Do you know how to feel His Presence, to experience the feeling that He is there not just in you, but beside you, before you, behind you, with you? Where you go, the Lord goes; where you walk, He walks. Your hand rests always in His your steps are guided by Him. He is constantly with you, counselling, instructing and leading.

This sounds wonderful, doesn't it? It is a happy and glorious state of being and a blissful frame of mind for you to be in. However, such a state of mind or being cannot be bought or bartered across a counter. You have to work for it and I shall tell you how.

Now, you have so many relationships in your life with your parents, your spouse, your children, your friends, your teachers, etc. The most important relationship is, of course, the one with God, your relationship with Me. Just as your worldly relationships have been carefully cultivated, nurtured and fostered by you, the one with Me also has to be developed with the same care and love. You may not know it, but developing a relationship with Me is much easier than it is with human beings-because, I do not make unreasonable and selfish demands on you. I accept what you offer and never ask for more. Even if you do not give Me anything, I still love you. I do not expect anything from you. On My part, I am always eager and ready to shower you with all My love, grace and blessings, but you should have the ability to receive them. Can the sun pervade your house with its warmth and light if you keep all your doors and windows shut? There is water everywhere, but if you want a drink, you must have a cup or a tumbler, musn't you?

Therefore, my dear one, the first thing you should do is to prepare yourself to receive My Grace. I do not want you to confine your prayers and devotion to the four walls of your shrine room. I want you to bring Me into your daily life and fill every free waking moment with thoughts of Me. I want you to talk to Me happily and joyfully as you would to a friend. I want you to turn to Me for help and strength as you would to your father. I want you to turn to Me for comfort and solace as you would to your mother. I am all of them in one. Believe that I am present physically with you. You may not see Me but I am. Believing this, cultivate an intimate and close association with Me. I am there to share everything with you-your joy and sorrow, gain and loss, pleasure and pain.

Think of Me as a member of your household, as the Head of your family. Wherever you are, let Me be with you; wherever you go, take Me with you. Don't banish Me to the *Pooja* room! When you have your food, offer it to Me also. Tell Me your troubles, bring Me your problems. I am only too happy to solve them for you. I'll smoothen your path and help you over pits and pikes, if you turn to Me completely and absolutely. Place all your trust and confidence in Me and I shall never let you down. I'll take care of you and look after your interests. I will bear the burden of your welfare.

Whatever you do, think you are doing it for Me. Whatever activity or work you are engaged in, let part of your mind always dwell on Me. When your mind is not occupied with any work or task, let it be filled with *Namasmarana, Japa* or *Bhajan*. Better still, go on reciting *Sai Gayathri* in your mind. This is a very powerful *Manthra* and will create vibrations in you which will awaken My Divine Presence. It will fill you with peace, love and joy.

So this, my dear, is what I mean by practising the presence of God. If you go on doing this sincerely and steadfastly, then I have to respond. I shall respond.

I APPRECIATE IMPLICIT OBEDIENCE

I am the Divine *Sadguru* and My Word is Divine. Once you accept Me as your *Guru* you should accept My Word as law.

I have given everyone of you a free will-the will and the right to decide and choose what you want to do, the right to carry out your actions according to your decision and the right to claim the reward. This is all according to the natural law of free will. I will not and cannot, therefore, interfere with the free will of a person.

But, as My devotee, you have, of your own free will and choice, decided to surrender yourself to Me. You have surrendered the right to think, plan, choose, decide and perform. You have also surrendered the right to claim the reward of action. I have not asked or compelled you to do this. You have chosen this course, out of your own free will, uninfluenced by any other person and out of your abounding love for Me. You now say that you have no will of your own. "Every thing is yours", you say, "Let Thy will be done". This is, of course, the right thing for a true devotee. It is the correct attitude which is concurrent with total surrender. Others may find it difficult to accept such an attitude. To them, it may seem absurd, foolish, even insane. But you can take it from Me that there is no higher devotion than this.

It is not very easy to arrive at this attitude of "*Atma Arpan*" (self-surrender). It is easier for one to give up his wealth, riches, status, position, family, friends, etc. It is extremely difficult, however, to give up one's individual will and surrender the right of thought, word and action. But a sincere devotee will realize the wisdom of such a surrender and he will try his utmost to arrive at this attitude.

Merely achieving this attitude is not enough, however. It is only the beginning, the starting point. You have now to learn to apply this attitude to every aspect of your life. You have to put your surrender into action. How do you do this? The answer is quite simple-implicit obedience. You have to obey My Word without question, hesitation, doubt, suspicion or uncertainty. There should be cent per cent willingness and readiness on your part to do what I say, immediately and unflinchingly, without pause for consideration or calculation. Remember how Ekalavya cut off his thumb the instant *Dronacharya* demanded it of him as *Guru Dakshina*. He did not even pause to think that cutting off his thumb would affect his prowess at archery. His only thought was to fulfil the word of his *Guru* and so he acted at once. Such was his implicit love, respect, regard and trust. And such is the kind of implicit obedience that you should have too.

I am not just any *Guru*. I am your Divine *Sadguru*. I know what is best for you and when you should get it. Therefore, have the firm faith and confidence that whatever I will for you is only for your highest good. I have a certain plan for you and I will things to happen in accordance with that plan. So, when I tell you to do something, it is for a definite purpose. Never doubt this. I never say anything without a reason. Therefore, learn to carry out My Word with absolute trust and implicit obedience.

Yesterday, you came to Me in confusion, guilt and fear. You said that you had been forced to tell an untruth in order to uphold My instructions. You asked Me if you had done wrong and if you would have to pay for it. I'll answer this by asking you another question. Didn't *Yudhishtra* tell a lie on the battle-field at the instigation of *Krishna*? I'll tell you this-when a devotee utters an untruth in order to uphold *Dharma*, the Lord assumes full responsibility for the devotee's act. If something you say or do deviates from the path of *Sathya*, I shall bear the responsibility and absolve you from the sin of *Asathya* - provided, of course, that what you say or do is only for My sake and for carrying out My Word. This, naturally, does not mean that you can go around as you please, telling untruths and uttering falsehood, while convincing yourself blithely that the Lord has promised to take the responsibil-

116

ity of your actions. No, this is not correct and proper, and you should not deceive yourself in this way.

Sometimes, the situation becomes extreme and the circumstance so difficult that desperation to uphold My Word drives you to swerve from the path of truth. Even then, you should be careful that you do not hurt or wound anyone by your act or word. If you, as a last resort, are forced to adopt a devious course solely for My sake and for the sake of following My Word, then I shall not blame you or hold you guilty. Such an act done in the name of Sai and for upholding Sai's Word, becomes an act of *Naivedhya*. Your *Dharma* is to obey Me and I guarantee that you shall not suffer by it or because of it. When you place your entire trust in Me and carry out My wishes implicitly, do you think that I will allow you to do or say anything which will cause you harm or hurt? However, beware! For, who knows, I may be just testing you to see whether you will obey Me absolutely and unreservedly, without counting the cost!

Therefore, my dear, be rest assured that I shall not let anything hurt you when I have your implicit confidence and obedience. Have faith in My Will and in My Word and adhere to them with the firm conviction that they only promote your welfare and ensure your ultimate good. Let this conviction take firm root in your mind. Then you will never be afraid of carrying out My Word. You will never be afraid of facing any opposition to My Will. You will never be afraid of fighting for what is right, and for what is *Dharma*. For, whatever I will to happen is always right and always in accordance with *Dharma*.

ATTUNE YOURSELF TO ME

By constantly practising My Presence, you will be able to develop a very close and intimate relationship with Me. What I want for you, what I wish you to do becomes more and more clear to you because you will have gained the sensitivity to feel and know what My Will is.

How do you achieve this sensitivity? I'll tell you with the help of an example. Now, what are the things you need for the picture on your T.V. screen to be clear and vivid? You need an uninterrupted flow of current, of course. And then, you need an antenna and control buttons. If all these are adjusted and are in good working order, the image on the screen will be sharp and bright. In your relationship with Me, your love is the current, your mind is the antenna and your intellect is the control. Your intellect has many control buttons like discrimination, detachment, concentration, judgement etc. If all these are well adjusted and tuned, the picture you receive will be clear and vivid. If even one of them does not function properly, the picture will be dull, hazy and shaky.

With this in mind, the first and foremost thing for you to do is to examine your control buttons and ensure that they remain in good working order. You have to watch them and keep a constant check on them. In other words, *Right - Watch* is the secret formula of maintenance. Watch your words, actions, thoughts, character and heart. If all these are properly adjusted and tuned, no problem will arise regarding the picture on your screen. So, keep a regular and efficient *Watch*.

Sometimes, when weather conditions are inclement and adverse, the antenna does not receive the signals sent out by the T.V. station satisfactorily. Therefore, take care and see that your internal antenna, "*mind*", is not affected by undesirable company and connections, doubts, suspicions and uncertainties. Do not let it be swayed by the gusts of biases and prejudices. Do not let it get damaged or corroded by the winds of fortune and the gales of life. Let it be supple and pliant so that it will bend with the breeze and not break.

The current of love flows through you but sometimes it gets blocked or fluctuates because of emotional crises and upsets. To prevent this, stabilise the current by maintaining a steady and regular voltage through unwavering faith, trust and confidence. The power of devotion is very high. Nothing can break it or cut it off.

So, my dear, this is the way in which you should maintain your inner screen or inner vision, If all the controls are in perfect working condition, the picture received on your inner screen will be perfect too. Then you will feel close to Me, you will have a feeling of oneness, togetherness and closeness. There will be perfect affinity and attunement between us. Your intuition will be sharpened to such a high extent that you will automatically know what actions, words and thoughts of yours will please Me, what I want you to be, what I want you to do and so on.

Some of you have the ability of inner communication with Me. You are able to ask Me directly for advice, guidance and instructions. Such an ability is not a boon or a gift from the Gods. It is something which you yourself have achieved and refined over a number of years and, perhaps over a number of births. This ability lies in each and every person and is only waiting to be discovered and developed. It is like a diamond which lies buried for years under layers of dirt, grime and dust. If these layers are removed, the true lustre is revealed. So, if you are not able to have inner communication now, don't think you can never have it. You can start cultivating it right from this moment by practising silence for a while every day. I have already told you that the Voice of God can be heard only when the heart and mind are silent. So, practise inner silence every day. When the mind is silent, My words flash across your mental screen in the form of thought waves. Problems get solved, ideas are resolved. What is this but the voice and work of God?

Therefore, attune yourself to Me, my dear. Your tuning system should be so fine and sensitive that you will be able to capture every subtle nuance and inflexion in My Word and Will. So, tune yourself. Raise your level of perception and intuition. Then you will be in constant contact with Me.

I AM ONLY A MIRROR

The ultimate truth is that you are divine. It is not merely that I am present in you. No, that is not all. The truth is that I am you and you are Me. The two of us are synonymous. There is no difference between us.

What do you see when you look into a mirror? You see your own reflection. It is only in the mirror that you can see yourself. If there is no mirror, you can't know what you are like, how you appear, what your features are etc. The mirror tells you what you are. Suppose the mirror is filmed with dust and dirt and is spotted and stained, what will the reflection be like? Will it be clear and vivid? No, it will be hazy, blurred and dimmed. If you clean the mirror and restore its shine, then you will be able to see a pure and perfect image.

It is the same in the case of you and Me also. I am but a mirror reflecting your innermost self. Your mirror right now is clouded with the mist of *Maya* (delusion) and is coated with the dust of *Ajnana* (ignorance). Hence you are unable to see a proper image and cannot see yourself for what you really are. You are actually divine, but you see yourself as something else-as ordinarily human and with human weaknesses, impurities, blemishes, desires and emotions.

Keep the mirror clean and shining bright. What is the result? You see your true reflection, your true image, your true self. You recognise yourself for what you really are. You see yourself as Sathchithananda, the embodiment of Truth, Knowledge and Bliss.

How should you keep the mirror clean and bright? You have to wash it with the soap of faith and the water of love. Wipe it dry with the cloth of detachment and polish it with the tissue of discrimination. You have to do this constantly and repeatedly. Even one little spot or stain on the mirror will spoil the perfection of the image.

Sometimes, you look at the mirror through the red lenses of anger, then the image seems distorted and ugly. At times, you wear the black lenses of despair and despondency, then the image looks dull and lifeless. If you look through the green lenses of envy and jealousy, the image will appear hideous and unattractive. However, if you have the pink lenses of love and the white lenses of equanimity, the image will be beautiful, radiant and glowing.

Do you know what actually happens when you are in a state of meditation and communion with Me? You think you receive messages and communications from Me but this is not really so. I cannot give you any knowledge. All the knowledge and wisdom in the universe are already present in you but are, unfortunately, obscured by the mists and fogs of delusion and egoism. That is why you are unable to grasp and understand the truth. What I do is merely clear the mist momentarily and disperse the fog for a while. Then you perceive a glimmer of the Truth, a flicker of the Reality. If just a fractional unveiling could impart such a wealth of wisdom, think how it would be if the entire curtain of *Maya* was to be lifted completely. The light of *Jnana* would burst upon you and you would become a fully realized and enlightened being.

You are now looking at yourself through the eyes of *Maya* and *Ajnana*. Instead, try to look at yourself through the eyes of *Sathya, Jnana* and *Prema*. The entire picture will seem different to you and you will perceive glimpses of divinity. Hence, my dear, scatter the clouds that are obscuring your vision, remove the webs that are impairing your sight, and try to wear "contact" lenses - the lenses which will give you a clear vision of yourself as divine, which will give you intimate contact, communion and oneness with Me!

AUM SHANTI SHANTI SHANTIH

AN ODE TO SAI

O' Beloved Lord Sai, so precious and dear,
You whom I most adore, worship and revere-
Your throne the world, Your home my hearth,
Your shrine ensconced in my humble heart.
Your graceful figure in orange silk so lustrous.
Your charming face, Your glorious hair so wondrous,
Your smile, Your word, so soft and sublime,
A dazzling Being with radiance most divine.
Your heavenly form does gladden and delight,
Dispel the gloom of misery and blight.
Your love my strength, Your sympathy my support,
Your grace my calm, Your kindness my comfort.
Ever my life companion and faithful help me,
My refuge lies at Your dainty Lotus Feet.
You lead me through time's shifting sands,
We walk together with entwined hands.
Over thorny briar and stony marshy land,
I tread in sweet content, guided by Your Divine Hand.

GLOSSARY

A
Adharma	:	Unrighteousness, that which is against the established code of conduct.
Ahimsa	:	Non-violence
Amrita	:	Nectar, ambrosia
Ananda	:	Joy, happiness, bliss.
Ananda Swaroopa	:	Embodiment of Bliss.
Anugraha	:	Divine Grace and Blessings.
Ardha	:	Half
Ardhangi	:	The god Shiva, husband.
Ardhangini	:	Man's better half, wife.
Arpan	:	Surrender, offering, entrusting.
Asathya	:	Untruth, falsehood.
Atma	:	Soul

B
Balam	:	Strength, energy power
Bhagavan	:	God
Bhajan	:	Song in praise of God.
Bhakta	:	Devotee or one who has love for God.
Bhakti	:	Devotion, attachment and love for God.
Bhava	:	Emotion, feeling
Bhojan	:	Food

127

D

Darshan	:	A sight or view of God
Daya	:	Compassion, kindness, mercy.
Dharma	:	Religion. Righteousness, code of conduct.
Dhyana	:	Meditation, contemplation
Divyatma Swaroopa	:	Embodiment of the Divine Soul or Divine Consciousness.

G

Guna	:	Quality, attribute, character
Guru	:	Master, teacher, guide. The word "*Guru*" means one who dispels ignorance.
Guru Dakshina	:	Remuneration or gift to the Master or spiritual preceptor.

J

Japa	:	Repetition or recitation of God's Name.
Jivatma	:	The individual soul.
Jnana	:	Knowledge, wisdom, enlightenment.

K

Karma	:	Action, duty; fate, destiny.
Karuna	:	Mercy, compassion, pity.
Katha	:	Story, tale.
Kripa	:	Kindness, mercy, favour
Krishna Paksha	:	The dark half of the month; the fortnight of the moon's waning.

M

Madhava	:	God
Manas	:	Mind
Manthra	:	A sacred hymn or prayer
Manava	:	Man, human being
Marga	:	Path, way
Mithya	:	Seemingly or apparently real, like a mirage
Mukthi	:	Liberation or freedom from bondage (from the cycle of birth and death).

N

Naivedhya	:	Offering to God at the time of worship.
Namasmarana	:	Contemplation of God's Name
Namavali	:	A collection of names describing and glorifying the divine nature and attributes of God
Nirvana	:	Liberation, highest bliss
Nishkama Karma	:	Action performed without the desire for reward.

P

Paramatma	:	The Universal, supra soul
Pooja	:	Worship
Prakriti	:	Nature
Prasadam	:	Consecrated and blessed food.
Prema	:	Love
Purusha	:	Man, male; God, the Supreme Being.

R

Rajas/Rajasic	:	Passionate, dynamic and active disposition which includes, qualities like egoism, arrogance anger, pride, conceit, etc.

S

Sadguru	:	The greatest Teacher or Master (God)
Sadhaka	:	One who is engaged in spiritual practice and discipline.
Sadhana	:	Spiritual practice and austerity; spiritual discipline.
Samsara	:	The gross, physical, material world.
Samskaras	:	One's collective thoughts, actions, qualities, character, morals, desires, ambitions etc. which one accumulates over a series of births.
Sannidhi	:	Refuge, nearness, shelter.
Sathchithananda	:	An exalted and divinely supreme state of being usually translated as Truth-Knowledge - Bliss.
Sathsang	:	The company of the good, the wise and the saintly.
Sathwa/Sathwic	:	Balanced, regulated and moderate disposition which includes qualities like equanimity, love, compassion, tolerance, generosity etc.

130

Sathya	:	Truth, Reality
Seva	:	Service, help, assistance
Sevak	:	One who renders service and help.
Shakti	:	Strength, energy, power. In Hindu philosophy Shakti is the consort of Lord Shiva. Shakti is the Goddess Parvathi, Durga, Kali.
Shanti	:	Peace, equanimity, tranquillity.
Shastras	:	Holy book, written principle or precept; any lawbook of the Hindus.
Shiva	:	The third God of the Hindu Trinity, the God of Destruction and Dissolution. In Yoga, Shiva represents cosmic consciousness. His consort is Shakti or Parvathi, the Goddess of Energy.
Shivam	:	Joy, auspicious
Sishya	:	Pupil, student, disciple.
Sloka	:	A verse or hymn in praise of God or any deity.
Stree	:	Woman, female
Sukla Paksha	:	The bright half of the month; the fortnight of the moon's waxing.
Sundaram	:	Beautiful, lovely, charming.
Swadharma	:	One's own duty or nature; duty which is natural to one's birth, occupation or position.

T

Tamas/tamasic	:	Dull, inactive and lethargic disposition which includes qualities like sloth, laziness, meanness, envy, jealousy etc.

U

Upanishads	:	Collectively called Vedanta, the Upanishads form the section of the Vedas which deal with the Higher Knowledge. The Upanishads were originally 1180 in number but through the centuries, many disappeared from human memory only 108 have now survived. Of these, 10 have attained popularity as a result of their depth and value.
Upavasa	:	Nearness or closeness to God.

V

Varshini	:	Showers
Vedas	:	They mean "Knowledge about everything" and are a collection of hymns and verses which originated from God Himself. There are four Vedas - Rig, Yajur Sama and Atharva, and are held as revealed scriptures by the Hindus.

Vichaara	:	Examination, inquiry, analysis.
Viveka	:	Discrimination, differentiation between right and wrong, truth and untruth, reality and unreality etc.

Y

Yogi	:	Ascetic, one who practises Yoga.

LOKA SAMASTHA SUKHINO BAVANTU

AUM SHANTI SHANTI SHANTIH

Also by the same Author :

1. THE SAI INCARNATION

A collection of personal experiences with the Divine Lord, Bhagavan Sri Sathya Sai Baba. It also contains expositions of the principles of Sathya, Dharma, Shanti, Prema and Ahimsa as propounded by Bhagavan.

2. SATHYA SAI's AMRITA VARSHINI

Nectarine showers of Truth and Spirituality from the Inner Sai.

3. BHAKTI SUDHA

Musings of a devotee on the sweetness of devotion.

BOOK REVIEWS

Sathya Sai's Amrita Varshini by Sudha Aditya
Published by Sai Towers Publishing, 3/497, Main Road,
Prasanthinilayam-515 134, India, pp.77, Rs.75/-

Bhagavan Baba's teachings are like nectar showers, drenching the inner spirit with love and bliss. The author received divine messages during her dhyana sessions. He guided her through the Inner Voice. He gave her elucidations on life, truth and spiritualism. When she prayed intensely to Bhagavan he confirmed the authenticity of the messages in a Dream Darshan.

She was lucky to keep a record of them. Now she presents the messages in the form of conversations with Bhagavan Baba. The compilation is arranged in ten chapters providing clarifications on ordinary spiritual exercises like Sathwic Food and Fasting to profound spiritual truths of Incarnation and Karmic Law.

Swami once explained to her the greatness of silence. When the mind is silent, the voice of God can be heard and you will have extra energy to think and work better.

Faith and confidence in God are inevitable concomitants that would act as a catalyst in the functioning of God's will and ushering in a new era. Faith refers to His Omnipresent, Omnipotent and Omniscient nature. Confidence refers to trust in His Word, Will and Work.

The basic criteria regarding food are its right quality and quantity. Along with food the basic discipline of speak no evil, see no evil, hear no evil and do no evil should be practised. Fasting in Sanskrit is Upavasa; which means living near God. A disciplined life is the surest way to reach us near God.

Swami explains the purpose of incarnation in memorable words. God always incarnates to demonstrate the unity of all religions and faiths and to establish a common brotherhood of man and Fatherhood of God.

The book reads as the quintessential Sai teachings.

A Compendium of the Teachings of Sathya Sai Baba
compiled by *Charlene Leslie-Chaden*.
Published by Sai Towers Publishing, 3/497, Main Road,
Prasanthinilayam-515 134, India, pp.739, Rs.555/-

The book under review is a single volume encyclopedic compilation of Sri Sathya Sai Baba's significant statements on varied subjects. The subjects range from child care to death and after death experiences. History, medicine, ethics, philosophy, administration, religion and spirituality - all find a place. Bhagavan Baba is an Avatar who transforms human life by transmuting ordinary life by the alchemy of the spiritual input. So everyone of his statements carries this Divine touch. More than 1,100 subjects have been identified and the definitive statements of Bhagavan Baba are quoted with relevant documentation of their sources. The special merit of the compilation is that recently published statements are preferred.

The quotations ring with authenticity and epigrammatic terseness. They have the force of incantations capable of transporting the reader to meditation.

Originally conceived as an educational resource guide for use in study circles, the book has grown to be a handy reference book or just a good inspirational read. Chance hitting of a passage will prove "a message for the day", an answer to a question or a solution to a problem.

The subjects are presented in alphabetical order which facilitates easy reference. A Sanskrit-to-English Glossary is also appended.

This is an invaluable resource book of Bhagavan Baba's Teachings placed at the service of students, teachers, research scholars, study groups and casual readers.

Books are despatched by Registered Book Post. Copies can be had by sending Money Order/International Money Order/Demand Draft drawn in favour of SRI SATHYA SAI TOWERS HOTELS PVT. LTD Payable at any Bank at Bangalore or Prasanthi Nilayam, addressed to Sai Towers, 3/497, Main Road, Prasanthi Nilayam - 515 134, India.

POSTAGE:- **India** :- At the rate of 50 ps. per 100 gms. plus Rs.6/- for Registration. Maximum 5 KG. Packing and Forwarding charges per parcel is Rs.40/-
Overseas:- 5 KGS by Sea Mail to North America, South America, Europe Rs.177/ Singapore, Malaysia, Australia etc. Rs.147/- plus packing and forwarding Rs.60/- per parcel.

NOTE:-

*THE PRICES SHOWN ABOVE WERE CORRECT AT THE TIME OF GOING TO PRESS, IT MAY DIFFER FROM THOSE PREVIOUSLY ADVERTISED.

A Story of India and Patal Bhuvaneshwar
by *Jennifer Warren*.

Published by Sai Towers Publishing, 3/497, Main Road, Prasanthinilayam -515 134, India, pp.76, Rs. 60/-

The book is her own account of a young American woman's travel in India. She had the privilege of meeting four spiritual Masters in India - - Dr. Goel,General Kant Taylor, Bhagavan Sri Sathya Sai Baba and Matha Amrithanandamayi. Avatars and saints, the writer says, are great catalysts to spark the divine bliss which exists within us.

Coming from a high-tech society, she experienced psychic shocks at the low-to-little tech rhythm of life in India. But long it was not after, when she identified the spiritual core of the Indian psyche. Her encounter with Shamji family helped her to a realization of spirituality in everyday life. She learned that it is in our nature to love,serve and be kind to each other. There was no substitute to this great experience. So she has come to hold India in great awe and esteem.

At Patal Bhuvaneshwar she had the vision of Lord Shiva moving towards her. The rituals in the cave temple saturated her with blissful vibrations and resulted in the integration of her physical,mental and spiritual states.

At Brindavan, Whitefield as Bhagavan Baba stood in front of her during darshan, she felt His energy flowed toward her. She also had very good darshans and very soothing interactions with Matha Amrithanandamayi. She was particularly touched by the effortless spirit of community of Indians during festive times. During Ammachi's birthday celebrations the Ashram at Vallickavu managed to feed and accommodate thousands of people on a plot of land that was only a few acres:

The narrative makes pleasant reading and the reader is bound to feel the relevance of pilgrimages as discovered by the writer.

Ashes, Ashes We all Fall Down by *Gloria St. John.*
Published by Sai Towers Publishing, 3/497, Main Road,
Prasanthinilayam - 515 134, India, pp. 99, Rs. 80/-

The book under review is, as its subtitle explains, an account
of how the writer became a devotee of Bhagavan Sri Sathya Sai
Baba and achieved great advancement in her spiritual life. She has
written it in the hope that it will be of assistance to fellow devotees to
strengthen their faith in the chosen path.

The writing was a spiritual sadhana that gave her an insight
into the process of her life, especially the painful parts of it. Her
education was through sufferings. Her indepth study of Bhagavan
Baba and His teachings did not help her to escape them but to bear
them with fortitude and wisdom. She had the inner realization that
crises in life are not a sign of her punishment or failings but the result
from her soul's contract with God to be purified.

Essentially a future-oriented person, she has now given up
all interest in planning. She awaits the Lord's bidding which manifests
through intuition, impulses, invitations and inspiration. Her conscience
has become her guide, leading her on the right path. At the tug of
guilt or anger, she stops and waits for guidance from within. A busy
person with many responsibilities, she is amazed at the quiet poise
and simple pace that her life has assumed in recent times. In the nine
chapters of the book, she records the process of her achieving this.

The book provides good explications of different aspects of
Devotion, Surrender, Dark Night of the Soul and Trust in the light of
Bhagavan Baba's teachings. Applying one by one, the writer was
helped to overcome the agony and despair that circled her from time
to time. It is heartening to read that she does not hold out any
specific formula for solving the riddle of existence. She, leaves it to
each enquirer to work his/her own way of salvation, by becoming
devotee of Bhagavan and realising what it implies - - a process in
God-ward march. Her life becomes a message for detaching oneself
from worldly suffering and orienting towards the greater purposes of
existence through devotion and service.

The book makes easy reading and impresses by its candour

OUR PUBLICATIONS

OUR PUBLICATIONS ...

38.SRI SATHYA SAI BABA YOUNG ADULTS PROGRAMME	- L.A. Ramdath	Rs. 80
39.SPIRITUAL IMPRESSIONS A BI-MONTHLY MAGAZINE		Rs.100
40.STUDY CIRCLES FOR DIVINITY	- Ross Woodward & Ron Farmer	Rs.390
41.THE PROPHECY	- Barbara Gardner	Rs.120
42.TEN STEPS TO KESAVA	- Johnima Wintergate	Rs.150
43.THY WILL BE DONE	- C.D. Mirchandani	Rs. 90
44.WAITING FOR BABA	- V. Ramnath	Rs. 95

FORTHCOMING PUBLICATIONS ...

01.ASHES,ASHES WE ALL FALL DOWN	- Gloria St. John
02.AT THE FEET OF SAI	- R. Lowenberg
03.ANANDA IS GOD	- K. Ramchandani
04.BHAGAVAN SRI SATHYA SAI BABA DISCOURSES IN KODAIKANAL APRIL - MAY 1997	- Pooja Kapahi
05.DIRECTORY OF MASTERS,SAINTS, ASHRAMS AND HOLY PLACES IN INDIA	- R.Padmanaban
06.DISCOVERING MARTIAL ARTS	- Deena Naidu
07.HINDU GODS AND GODDESSES : MAN COMPRISES ALL DEITIES A compilation of the Teachings of Bhagavan Sri Sathya Sai Baba	- Pooja Kapahi
08.HOLY MISSION DIVINE VISION	- Sai Usha
09.IN THE DEPTH OF SILENCE	- K. Ramchandani
10.KRISHNAMURTHI AND THE FOURTH WAY	- Evan Grans
11.LADDER	- Lightstorm
12.ROADS TO THE DIVINE	- P.P. Arya
13.SAI BABA - THE ETERNAL COMPANION	- B.P. Misra
14.SAI UPADESH	- Sai Usha
15.SAI DARSHAN	- Vimla Sahni
16.SAI's STORY	- Shaila Hattiangadi
17.SAI NAMAVALI	- Jagat Narain Tripathi
18.THE THOUSAND SONGS OF LORD VISHNU	- Jeannette Caruth
19.THE HEART OF SAI	- R. Lowenberg
20.THE GRACE OF SAI	- R. Lowenberg
21.THE OMNI PRESENCE OF SAI	- R. Lowenberg
22.YOGA THERAPY	- R. Lowenberg
23.SANSKRIT-ENGLISH- DICTIONARY	
24.ENGLISH BHAJANS	
25.INDIAN BHAJANS	